BCS
The Chartered Institute for IT

...anding

GW00392322

You may also be ...er ested in...

Problem Manager
The role of a problem manager is described in depth, from the required skills to processes, tools and standards.

978-1-78017-237-8

£19.99

Business Relationship Manager
An excellent introduction to this role which is central to all aspects of an organisation's interaction with customers.

978-1-78017-250-7

£19.99

IT Service Management
This guide introduces ITIL and offers a practical understanding of IT service management.

978-1-906124-93-9

£20.99

www.bcs.org/bookshop

BC852/LD/AD/0614

SERVICE DESK
AND INCIDENT
MANAGER

BCS, THE CHARTERED INSTITUTE FOR IT

BCS, The Chartered Institute for IT, champions the global IT profession and the interests of individuals engaged in that profession for the benefit of all. We promote wider social and economic progress through the advancement of information technology science and practice. We bring together industry, academics, practitioners and government to share knowledge, promote new thinking, inform the design of new curricula, shape public policy and inform the public.

Our vision is to be a world-class organisation for IT. Our 70,000 strong membership includes practitioners, businesses, academics and students in the UK and internationally. We deliver a range of professional development tools for practitioners and employees. A leading IT qualification body, we offer a range of widely recognised qualifications.

Further Information
BCS The Chartered Institute for IT,
First Floor, Block D,
North Star House, North Star Avenue,
Swindon, SN2 1FA, United Kingdom.
T +44 (0) 1793 417 424
F +44 (0) 1793 417 444
www.bcs.org/contact

http://shop.bcs.org/

SERVICE DESK AND INCIDENT MANAGER

Careers in IT service
management

Peter Wheatcroft

Published by BCS Learning & Development Ltd, a wholly owned subsidiary of BCS The Chartered Institute for IT First Floor, Block D, North Star House, North Star Avenue, Swindon, SN2 1FA, UK.
www.bcs.org

Paperback ISBN: 978-1-78017-233-0
PDF ISBN: 978-1-78017-234-7
ePUB ISBN: 978-1-78017-235-4
Kindle ISBN: 978-1-78017-236-1

Ebook available

British Cataloguing in Publication Data.
A CIP catalogue record for this book is available at the British Library.

Disclaimer:
The views expressed in this book are of the author(s) and do not necessarily reflect the views of the Institute or BCS Learning & Development Ltd except where explicitly stated as such. Although every care has been taken by the author(s) and BCS Learning & Development Ltd in the preparation of the publication, no warranty is given by the author(s) or BCS Learning & Development Ltd as publisher as to the accuracy or completeness of the information contained within it and neither the author(s) nor BCS Learning & Development Ltd shall be responsible or liable for any loss or damage whatsoever arising by virtue of such information or any instructions or advice contained within this publication or by any of the aforementioned.

Typeset by Lapiz Digital Services, Chennai, India.

MIX
Paper from
responsible sources
FSC® C013604

CONTENTS

LIST OF FIGURES AND TABLES

ABOUT THE AUTHOR

Peter Wheatcroft is a specialist in service transformation and has consulted widely in this area since 2002. He has worked actively with many blue-chip companies to improve the management of their IT departments leading to the achievement of flagship service standards, and these assignments have underpinned the advice and guidance contained in this book.

Before becoming a consultant, Peter was Director of Commercial and Information Management for Alliance & Leicester plc, where his responsibilities encompassed the business management of Information Services including financial, supplier and technology partnerships and the attainment of World Class status for IT services and processes. Prior to that, he was the Director of Technology Services responsible for integrating operational IT activities of the different group businesses – Alliance & Leicester, Girobank and Sovereign Finance – into a coherent unit that was externally benchmarked as 'best practice' – including three CIB awards and commendations for technological achievement – and also acknowledged by management, customers and staff. Until 1986, Peter was responsible for developing and delivering IT and IS services for the NCB South Yorkshire Area.

He has a BSc in Electrical and Electronic Engineering and is both a Chartered Engineer and a Chartered IT Professional, holding fellowships awarded by the IET, BCS and the CMI. He has been an active contributor to the SFIA and ISM career and skills development schemes for BCS and is an approved CITP membership assessor, becoming one of the first BCS members to gain the new Certificate of Current Competence. He is also a Moderator for the UK IT Industry Awards, having worked on these in various roles since 2002.

His papers and articles have been published in a number of trade journals such as *Service Talk, Computer Weekly, The Computer Bulletin* (now *ITNOW*), *Support World, Bios Magazine, Computing Business* and *The Times*. His book, *World Class IT Service Delivery* (ISBN 978-1-902505-82-4,) was published by BCS in 2007.

ACKNOWLEDGEMENTS

I would like to thank a number of people for their support and encouragement in helping me to write this book, and in particular:

Paul Cash of Partners in IT for permission to use extracts from their GovernIT process model, and John Perks for the diagrams that explain it.

Justin Loftas and John Griffiths for their enthusiasm in being able to describe what it means to work as a service desk manager in big companies.

Carole Ratcliffe FCIPD for work on the customer journey and the personal characteristics needed for someone to be selected into a service desk role.

All figures and tables are the work of the author except for the following:

Figure 3.8 is courtesy of Carole Ratcliffe
Figures 4.2 and 4.3 are courtesy of John Perks
Figure 5.1 was created by Roy Shepherd

Thanks are also extended to the following organisations who have allowed extracts of their material to be used in this book. These organisations are:

BCS, The Chartered Institute for IT
The SFIA Foundation
AXELOS

It is acknowledged that ITIL® is the copyright © of AXELOS Limited 2011. All rights reserved. Material is reproduced with the permission of AXELOS.

Extracts from SFIA are reproduced by kind permission of the SFIA Foundation.

REFERENCES AND WEB LINKS

The BCS CPD portal can be found on:

http://bcs.org/cpd

The syllabus for the BCS Specialist Certificate in Service Desk and Incident Management is on:

http://certifications.bcs.org/upload/pdf/itsm-sdim-syllabus.pdf

ABBREVIATIONS AND DEFINITIONS

ABBREVIATIONS

ACD	automatic call distribution (system)
API	application programming interfaces
ATM	automated teller machine
BAU	business as usual
BCS	BCS, The Chartered Institute for IT
BMP	best management practice
BYOD	bring your own device
CAB	Change Advisory Board
CITP	Chartered IT Professional
CMDB	configuration management database
CMI	Chartered Management Institute
CMIS	configuration management information system
CMMI	Capability Maturity Model Integration
COBIT	Control Objectives for Information Technology
CPD	continuing professional development
CSI	continual service improvement
DSS	deliver, service and support
FOI	The Freedom of Information Act
HR	human resources

ICT	information and communications technology
IET	The Institution of Engineering and Technology
ISACA	Information Systems Audit and Control Association
ISM	information security management
IT	information technology
ITIL	IT Infrastructure Library
ITMG	IT management
ITOP	IT operations
ITSM	IT service management
IVR	interactive voice response
KPI	key performance indicator
MCSE	Microsoft Certified Solutions Expert
MBA	Master of Business Administration
MOT	moments of truth
NOS	National Occupational Standards for Management and Leadership
NVQ	National Vocational Qualification
OLA	operational level agreement
PA	personal assistant
RCB	registered certification body
SDIM	service desk and incident manager (or management)
SFIA	Skills Framework for the Information Age
SFIAplus	A value-add extension to the SFIA framework from BCS
SIG	special interest group
SLA	service level agreement
SLM	service level management

SLT	service level target
SMS	service management system
SVQ	Scottish Vocational Qualification
USUP	SFIA code for the SDIM skills
VIP	very important person

DEFINITIONS

Skill A recognisable area of IT competence within the workplace

Task A skill being exercised at a particular level in the organisation

Level Measure of the degree of responsibility that an IT job possesses

Role The set of responsibilities and activities performed by a job. One person may exercise different roles, for example Incident Management and Request Fulfilment, in order to do their job

1 THE CONTEXT FOR THIS BOOK

INTRODUCTION

Service is not the same as a product. Unlike a manufactured article, service cannot be mass-produced, pre-packaged and sold through different channels – it always involves the customer and the provider in a very specific, real-time relationship. And also unlike a manufactured article, service cannot be disassociated from its supplier as it involves actual dialogue, which is why service management is a largely misunderstood part of the IT delivery chain. It is often confused with IT operations (ITOP) and sometimes derided as being the province of back-room staff, yet frequently represents the greatest proportion of IT customer complaints when its delivery does not match customer expectations.

These expectations might not be capable of being satisfied by an existing service desk team, which is why setting achievable levels of performance at the outset is a vital part of the IT service-delivery cycle. Since service involves the customer and the provider in an interactive transaction, there needs to be a shared understanding of what a good outcome will look like. This book has been written in order to explore the people dimension of the three primary attributes of an IT service as shown below:

- people;
- process;
- products.

A simplistic view of these three attributes could lead to the conclusion that Service = People + Process + Products with similar weightings – a third each.

However, users of an IT service will normally expect processes and technology to work properly all the time and will only contact the service provider, through the service desk, when things go wrong. This is often a distress situation and the way in which user issues are dealt with is vitally important to the achievement of customer satisfaction because, if the customer trusts and is positive about how the service desk works, this will reflect well on the overall IT organisation. In this case, the people aspect – which is the ongoing service relationship – is of greater importance to the user than the design of the service itself as it is a more immediate concern.

This suggests that the weighting between the three attributes of service is not a simplistic equation of thirds. Instead, the achievement of customer satisfaction, which should always be the aim of an IT function, is rather more skewed to the people dimension than the others, which are usually addressed at a different part of the service lifecycle – the design stage. So, the weightings we will be exploring in this book look more like:

Service = ½ × People (i.e. 50%) + ¼ × Process (i.e. 25%) + ¼ × Products (i.e. 25%)

This is not to downplay the role of published standards and frameworks and how the many good technology solutions available to the IT buyer can be used for business benefit. Rather, the solutions aspect has been emphasised to a remarkable extent in recent years – almost to the point where vendors would have you believe that the act of buying their product will solve your problem without taking the ongoing management into account. However, this approach is rather like buying a car and not accepting that it needs to be serviced – and yet the likelihood of buying another car of the same make will depend heavily on the after-sales service that is received.

Operational reality shows just how much of a problem this type of thinking can be in service management, as the promises of best practice processes falter in the light of incomplete implementation, and technology solutions that have been bought at considerable expense often rely on teams without the skills or resource levels to make them work properly. The following chapters explore and explain why the people aspects of the service equation are so crucial to the management of IT services and should not be regarded as a product.

For those who already work in or are looking to work in an incident management role, or aspire to become a service desk manager, this book describes what is needed in order to do well in the job. If you are a consultant or product supplier, then the roles and characteristics described in this book will help you to ensure that the inheritors of any process or technology implementation you are responsible for will have the skills and personal attributes to properly manage what is delivered. This is not just in their interest but also your own, as a poor ongoing service experience will reflect as badly on the product as it will on the people charged with delivering it.

This book describes roles that make up the function of service desk and incident management and how they relate to other jobs in IT. A few important definitions are introduced here concerning the terminology associated with this function.

- A skill is a recognisable area of competence within the workplace.
- A task is the exercise of a skill at a particular level in the organisation.
- A level is a measure of the degree of responsibility a job possesses.
- A role is defined as the set of responsibilities and activities performed by a job. One person may exercise different roles, for example incident management and request fulfilment, in order to do their job.

The roles that will be covered in this book are those normally carried out by staff working on a service desk – namely, incident management, request fulfilment, access management and, in some cases, other duties as well. A service desk is often a large function, sometimes amounting to hundreds of people if support is being provided to many different subsidiaries or for an international user base. It offers a varied workload across what is sometimes a 24-hour day with peaks and troughs of demand that need careful management to maintain an acceptable level of responsiveness to the people who depend on the function to fix their issues. There are references in each chapter to the different levels of job that make up a service desk as well as the different types of work that they are involved in.

However, no one in IT works in isolation – there are nearly 100 skills defined for the IT industry, and that of service desk and incident management (SDIM) is one of them. The SDIM function is the one in IT that everyone within a business or the external customer base, depending on business type, will be aware of for the simple reason that it is responsible for handling everyday IT issues. This is why it is so important: because the level of customer contact that arises from dealing with thousands of incidents every week or month far exceeds the customer contact potential from any other IT job.

It is this degree of contact with the customer that defines the service desk's importance to the overall customer proposition of an IT department – and yet this critical role is often overlooked by IT directors as it is not high enough on their strategic radar. This is a mistake: if customers do not rate the everyday service highly enough, they are unlikely to be enthusiastic about project or design capabilities, which are usually regarded as discretionary activities. Providing service day in and day out is classed as 'keeping the lights on' and the combined cost of data centres, networks and desktop support can account for more than half the overall IT operational expenditure, although this is not just in managing incidents. It is obvious that the ongoing management of service needs to be done efficiently, effectively and in a way that is regarded as value-adding rather than as an afterthought.

What closes this introduction are two important features: that of **best practice** and **professionalism**. The reason these are introduced is to explain that how an SDIM function operates is very important in relation to its industry peer group. Your own organisation, and others in the IT industry, will use external points of reference and, as both terms will be encountered in the workplace, it is appropriate to explain them at this stage. They should be regarded and understood as foundations, or building blocks, for your work.

Best practice can be defined in a number of ways, most commonly by the demonstration of consistently good results that can be verified by external benchmarks. However, best practice as a term is overused and can be mistaken for something that implies 'best of the best', which is incorrect as this is actually what 'world class' represents. So another way of understanding types of practice is to regard use of the term 'best practice' as meaning good practice, which it certainly is. There are a number of formal definitions of best practice that can be referred to, such as the term 'proven activities or processes that have been successfully used by multiple organisations' used by ITIL (IT Infrastructure Library). Whether practices have been verified as good by comparative benchmarking or whether they deliver superior results are both important aspects for the results orientation and attributes of jobs in service desk and incident management.

One of the key ways of demonstrating good practice is to be regarded as a leader in service delivery and being asked, for example, to host special interest groups or by speaking at seminars. This usually results from the reputation created when, for instance, a practitioner is asked to present what they have achieved at a conference following a successful project implementation, or by writing a case study for a professional journal. Such presentations and articles can result from being a member of a special interest group (SIG) or a user forum where ideas and notes on how to deal with particular issues can be compared and discussed with peers.

The other important term to draw out at this stage is that of professionalism. A professional is someone who has undertaken structured education and training in a particular discipline and can therefore be expected to be proficient in the job that is being done, the standard of which will depend on the level at which you are operating. BCS, The Chartered Institute for IT – referred to from here on as just BCS – treats professionalism very seriously by publishing SFIA*plus*, the IT skills, training and development standard, and through the provision of certifications spanning the SFIA (Skills Framework for the Information Age) framework. This is supported by the availability of tools to manage CPD (Continuing Professional Development) tracking so that people can understand what they need in order to succeed at their current level, and what the skills, attributes and experience needs are at other levels. So, when the term 'professional' is used, it can be understood in the context of someone who has been trained to use the skills for which they are employed.

The way in which people can follow a career on a service desk, and how they can achieve the necessary qualifications using CPD, is covered in Chapter 5. This includes material that has never before been drawn together into a single publication, such as the personal qualities necessary to succeed in these roles, as well as how interviewers will be interested in finding out whether someone can do the job they are applying for. This book complements the BCS Specialist Certificate in SDIM, and, for anyone looking to improve their chances of succeeding in this type of job, interviews with two very successful service desk managers have been included in Chapter 6.

2 AN OVERVIEW OF SERVICE DESK AND INCIDENT MANAGEMENT

INTRODUCTION TO IT SERVICE MANAGEMENT

All SDIM functions, roles and processes fall under the discipline of IT service management, or ITSM for short. ITSM forms an essential part of an IT department's overall remit to manage the information assets of the organisation it serves. It sits alongside the disciplines of systems development and business analysis, and others, depending on how the work is structured. ITSM provides both the day-to-day operational services needed to run business systems and manage their use as well as the advice and guidance needed to ensure that new services are designed in the most effective and efficient way possible.

ITSM has two main areas of focus: to manage services provided to the existing customer base to agreed standards, and to work with other IT functions to integrate new applications into the catalogue of existing services that they will run alongside. It therefore faces outwards to the customer through the provision of services such as a help desk, a training function and hardware maintenance, and internally to the IT department through the provision of technical expertise.

Some or all of these activities may be provided by specialist third-party organisations rather than by an in-house team, but the discipline is the same regardless of which agency actually does the work. No matter whether it is an external or in-house function, ITSM is owned by the IT department and is controlled by means of both internal and external service level agreements. It is measured by such means as customer satisfaction surveys, business throughput and the attainment of various quality and performance targets.

The following four brief statements summarise what ITSM means and how it influences the jobs we are concentrating on in this book:

THE CONTEXT FOR ITSM

1. A service is a means of delivering value to customers by facilitating outcomes customers want to achieve without the ownership of specific costs and risks.
2. Service management is a set of specialised organisational capabilities for providing value to customers in the form of services.
3. Organisational capabilities include all the processes, methods, functions, roles and activities used by a service provider to enable them to deliver services to customers.
4. Service operation is where the value of a service is realised.

If we look at statement 3, we can see that ITSM is a collection of capabilities that encompass the skills of people as well as processes and tool deployment in order to manage a service. Statement 4 is important in explaining that nothing that precedes it has any value unless service operations are executed consistently and to an agreed standard, and the achievement of customer satisfaction is paramount. As service management jobs face the customer, it is obviously important to make sure that how services are managed always meets their needs and expectations.

ITSM has to be a very structured discipline with well documented procedures and controls in order to perform consistently at the required level. This has led to the development of several frameworks and standards designed to help an ITSM function structure their activities in ways that help to achieve the desired results. These frameworks are also used by both internal and external auditors as an objective way to assess conformance with management control requirements, which is important to every organisation that has to comply with, for example, the Data Protection Act and other legislation. These control requirements are more stringent in a regulated industry, such as banking, where national supervision is a government requirement and IT controls are routinely inspected. Some examples of mature frameworks for ITSM are introduced here, as anyone working in this field needs to understand how their work will be controlled and measured.

The Best Management Practice (BMP) portfolio managed by AXELOS, the joint venture company who are responsible for ITIL as well as PRINCE2, sits alongside COBIT (Control Objectives for Information Technology) as the two most widely used governance frameworks in the world. Both emphasise the degree to which ITSM needs to be governed and controlled and there are detailed process definitions contained within each framework. These are very similar to each other, so a reference in one framework will almost certainly exist in the other. COBIT is used more extensively in the US than the rest of the world, whereas ITIL is used heavily everywhere outside the US but also by some multinational corporations with interests both in the US and elsewhere.

A further framework that is relevant to ITSM is SFIA. It is concerned with skills and competencies, where individuals can learn about the different roles that exist in IT and what skills are needed for them. Equally, organisations use this framework extensively to support the design of their IT departments and to assess what training, development and other forms of intervention are needed to maintain the appropriate level of skills in the workforce. SFIA is an independent publication supported by a number of strategic partners known as Foundation Members, of which BCS is one.

ITSM is one of six categories of IT job defined by SFIA, which, for the sake of completeness, are shown in Table 2.1 with the number of skills each one contains:

Table 2.1 A breakdown of the IT skills described within SFIA

IT job category	Number of different skill types
Strategy and Architecture	23
Business Change	20
Solution Development and Implementation	18
Service Management (ITSM)	21
Procurement and Management Support	9
Client Interface	5

Together, these six categories define all the 96 IT skills that make up an IT competency, of which service management represents over 20 per cent.

Reference will be made to all three of these frameworks throughout this book in order to provide readers with an industry view and to ensure that the language and terminology used are consistent with external standards.

One feature of the roles described in this book needs to be explained here as it will be referred to in several other chapters. Service Desk is a **function** of an IT department as it consists of teams that use processes, procedures and technology as required in order to correctly achieve objectives. Incident management, however, is a **process** used by a service desk in order to bring consistency to the way in which individual incidents are handled and so is one of the activities managed by the service desk. A function is therefore an organisational entity whereas a process is a collection of activities, and this is an important distinction. When we refer to incident management we are thinking of the process and when we refer to a service desk then we are thinking of the organisational aspects that encompass process responsibilities. Figure 2.1 shows the five operational processes that have been defined within the Service Operation lifecycle.

Figure 2.1 Operational processes defined by ITIL

Processes in the Service Operation phase of the ITIL® Service Lifecycle
Event Management
Incident Management
Request Fulfilment
Problem Management
Access Management

So, whilst the service desk does not exist as a process in the ITIL framework, it will use the processes that are shown in Figure 2.1.

We have already defined a function as a team of people and the tools they use to carry out one or more processes or activities, and a process as being a structured set of activities designed to achieve a specific objective. A service desk will typically draw heavily on the processes of incident management, request fulfilment and, very often, access management in order to discharge its purpose, and so it can be seen that the job of a service desk manager has breadth as well as focus. The same goes for staff working on a service desk as they often need to be able to work with any of the processes in the Service Operation lifecycle, which use different scripts in order to discharge their objectives. The differences in job scope between the three types of process operated by service desk personnel are explored in subsequent chapters, but what needs to be understood at this stage is that the service desk manager in high-performing organisations will usually be nominated as the process manager for both the incident management and request fulfilment processes and so is responsible for determining how well they run and will be accountable for the results. This responsibility may be separate from the role of process owner, for example if an organisation has more than one function doing the same work in different parts of the world under different managers, but the two roles – of owner and manager – are most often assigned to the same individual. The attributes needed of process owners and managers are described further in Chapter 3.

Figure 2.1 describes just five processes as being the responsibility of the Service Operation competency of the overall ITIL service lifecycle, and yet there are many skills needed to operate these processes properly. Having the required skills, but working only on a 'best endeavours' basis, does not bring consistent results, in the same way that working with a best practice process but not having the right skills will not do so either.

There are, in total, 21 service management skills involved in the overall service lifecycle and, of these, 11 are aligned to Service Operation. These include the skills of SDIM that we are concentrating on, and it is important to understand at this stage how jobs on a service desk relate to the overall IT department as well as to the service delivery discipline within which they work. A variety of skills are needed to deal with the activities involved in service provision, and the interplay between skills, processes and activities is a key part of what makes up any specialist function. Table 2.2 summarises the full range of service management skills including SDIM.

It is not necessary at this stage to be concerned with what all the detail in this table means as the relevant parts will be explained in the following chapters. However, it should be understood that the four broad categories of skill – strategy, design, transition and operation – relate to the four key stages

Table 2.2 Service management skills contained within the SFIA framework

Category	Service Management Skills	Code	Level						
			1	2	3	4	5	6	7
Service strategy	IT management	ITMG					5	6	7
	Financial management for IT	FMIT				4	5	6	
Service design	Capacity management	CPMG				4	5	6	
	Availability management	AVMT				4	5	6	
	Service level management	SLMO		2	3	4	5	6	7
Service transition	Service acceptance	SEAC				4	5	6	
	Configuration management	CFMG		2	3	4	5	6	
	Asset management	ASMG				4	5	6	
	Change management	CHMG		2	3	4	5	6	
	Release and deployment	RELM			3	4	5	6	
Service operation	System software	SYSP			3	4	5		
	Security administration	SCAD			3	4	5	6	
	Radio frequency engineering	RFEN		2	3	4	5	6	
	Application support	ASUP		2	3	4	5		
	IT operations	ITOP	1	2	3	4			
	Database administration	DBAD		2	3	4	5		
	Storage management	STMG			3	4	5	6	
	Network support	NTAS		2	3	4	5		
	Problem management	PBMG			3	4	5		
	Service desk & incident management	USUP	1	2	3	4	5		
	IT estate management	DCMA			3	4	5	6	

Reproduced by kind permission of the SFIA Foundation.

of the service management lifecycle but do not include a fifth, which is CSI (continual service improvement). CSI draws contributions from the entire range of IT disciplines rather than needing specific lifecycle skills. Service management skill types exist at several different levels from 1 to 7, where 7 is the most senior level defined for a specific skill and 1 is the most junior. There are two Level 7 jobs in service management – IT Management (ITMG) and Service Level Management (SLM) – and, with the exception of ITOP, which covers the tasks of day-to-day activities connected with routine operations, all the other skills extend to at least Level 5. We will be looking more closely at the characteristics of these seven levels in Chapter 3 and so, at this stage, it is enough to understand that there is a wide spread.

However, this is not a book about the overall field of ITSM and neither is it about ITIL, COBIT or other frameworks, and so the focus will now narrow to the world of service desks and incident management. More particularly, the emphasis will be on the people aspects of these areas, and whilst processes and tools will be referenced from time to time, they are not the reason this book exists – which may be a relief to readers as there are many good books about such matters and it would be repetitive to reproduce their content.

SERVICE DESK AND INCIDENT MANAGEMENT WITHIN IT SERVICE MANAGEMENT

It can be seen from Table 2.2 that SDIM – or USUP, as SFIA prefers to label it – is one of the 21 skills belonging to service management and one of 11 within service operations. It is interesting to note that, in terms of organisation design, many companies align their service desk and incident teams not to the operations teams but to user-facing ones such as a customer services department. This is quite acceptable, providing the processes and supporting workflow cross organisational boundaries seamlessly. However, it can sometimes be apparent that this is where discontinuities appear, though it is understandable that an organisational segregation between technical management and customer management will frequently exist. This is because the activities of operations teams, who are technically focused on such things as servers and networks, and those people who face the customer need different skills. But, regardless of how an organisation is designed, the overall service delivery chain must encompass all the components necessary to deliver the customer proposition regardless of which particular skills are needed. Technical staff in operational specialisms, or third-party suppliers working without reference to the customer team, can inadvertently cause considerable difficulties for their service desk counterparts, which is why they must be included in, and managed by, the incident management process. Techniques, such as Moments of Truth (MOT), exist to align cause with effect and will be referenced in Chapter 3 as methods that service desk staff can use to bring a range of technical colleagues into the overall service chain, and hence control remedial actions that may affect customers.

Organisation design is clearly an area where the employing company will have a view as to how it is best achieved. The frameworks already mentioned can be used as sources of advice and guidance when arriving at a preferred outcome, although it can be said that there are few companies who organise their teams strictly along the lines of the four lifecycle categories of Strategy, Design, Transition and Operation. In the same way, few companies organise their teams along the four COBIT management domains of Plan, Build, Run and Monitor despite the widespread nature of the publications available for both these best practice frameworks. In this book, we will focus on what makes a good SDIM person regardless of the organisational boundaries that may act either for or against concerted management control of the activities they are involved in. A good service desk manager will be able to influence behaviours and activities in the wider IT department within which they work in terms of both their functional contribution and their professional authority.

A service desk is designed to be the primary point of contact between the provider of an IT service and its customers. In an ideal world it would be the sole point of contact, but incomplete implementation of processes aligned with less than optimum staffing levels and skills issues sometimes mean that customers will bypass the official helpline and go direct to the person or team they believe will best be able to resolve their issue. Whilst this is rarely documented, my experience of analysing incident management activities carried out in many different companies suggests that between 10 per cent and 20 per cent of all incident resolutions do not originate from actions taken by the service desk. There are various reasons why this is the case, although there are five main themes which come up repeatedly in large companies.

REASONS CUSTOMERS GIVE FOR CIRCUMVENTING THE SERVICE DESK

1. The service desk is not perceived to have the skills to resolve the reported incident without referral to someone in a different team.
2. The helpline number is often too busy, leading to long waiting times.
3. Service desk staff do not add value, as they only log and escalate calls.
4. Incident management is seen as a technical, not procedural activity.
5. Customers like to receive immediate attention even for minor issues and the service desk prioritisation mechanisms do not cater for these.

All these reasons can be regarded as valid if the SDIM resources are not properly allocated, or performing at an appropriate level, and so this is what we are interested in addressing. The value of seeing a service desk fulfilling the design intent of being the single point of contact with customers, and managing all incidents within agreed service levels, is the ambition that everyone in SDIM should aim to achieve, and it is a key organisational quality metric.

SERVICE DESK AND INCIDENT MANAGEMENT IN PRACTICE

We have already explained that there is a difference between the emphasis of a service desk – the function – and incident management – the process. As the service desk manager is most often designated as the process owner for incident management, this distinction does not often give rise to conflicts of interest. By way of example, the extract in Table 2.3, taken from a real job description for a service desk manager, illustrates the emphasis that needs to be given to process management as well as task management.

Table 2.3 Some responsibilities of a real service desk manager

Responsibilities	Key tasks	% of time spent
Develops and implements the strategy, standards and procedures within which the IT Service Desk will operate.	• Create the Service Desk strategy. • Develop, own and maintain the Incident Management process. • Develop, own and maintain the Major Incident process. • Develop, gain agreement to and maintain the Escalation procedures. • Develop and manage the performance KPIs.	5%

(Continued)

17

Table 2.3 (Continued)

Responsibilities	Key tasks	% of time spent
	• Create the framework for the documentation of standards and ensure adherence.	
	• Operate the Access Management process as defined by ISM.	
	• Develop and maintain the Service Request process.	
	• Develop and own Customer Service standards against which all Service Desk personnel will be measured.	
	• Manage the Knowledge Base and ensure that support documentation is developed for business applications and for the Service Desk personnel to enable customers and staff to do their respective jobs.	

The time allocation shown here presumes that some form of transformation project will have developed the base procedures and handed them over to the service desk manager for further enhancement and maintenance. However, the percentage of time spent on developing and implementing processes can make up as much as 25 per cent of the total working week if the service desk manager is charged with the responsibility for developing these processes themselves, which is not usually the case in my experience. The operational demands of running a busy service desk do not normally allow a manager to also develop a new operating model, which is seen as a project responsibility. What can also be seen from the task breakdown is that the manager has the lead responsibility for customer service which includes such things as the operational KPIs (key performance indicators) by which the contribution of the desk will be assessed and staff performance will be measured.

Staff working on a service desk can perform several different roles depending on the work assignment they are given. As the highest volume of work will come from answering calls from customers relating to an issue being experienced with an IT service, most of the time that staff spend at work will be on the task of incident management. This work ranges from initially learning of an incident by telephone, by email or other electronic means or even by face-to-face contact depending on how the service has been set up.

The initial point of contact for any of the methods of being notified of a service-affecting incident is known as a tier 1 resource – meaning the person who handles routine queries where the emphasis needs to be on time to answer, call logging and speed of resolution. Typical actions at tier 1 will involve such activities as password resets, dealing with maintenance requests for, say, a replacement keyboard, resolving common desktop issues and perhaps even restarting workgroup servers. Other tasks involve handling calls rejected from the queue using an ACD (automatic call distribution) system, although this often tends to be done at supervisory level as an abandoned call may involve an irate customer. Tier 1 staff will typically also be responsible for managing access requests and requisitions, such as ordering printer consumables or a replacement mobile phone charger for a user who has lost one, from a catalogue of commodity items.

Backing up this frontline team will be tier 2 staff, who will have greater technical skills and so act in particular specialisms such as desktop application support, network issues or dealing with a range of 'how do I?' queries. They may act as escalation from tier 1 staff, in which case they can be expected to deal with, and to achieve, resolution of a particular customer issue during a single phone call, which is how most customers want the service to work. Whilst this is an ideal situation, it is sometimes not going to be the case as they may need to research the issue and call the customer back, in which case the response needs to be time bound in order to maintain customer confidence. If the issue is service-affecting, then the response from either tier 1 or tier 2 will be as an incident manager, and they will be responsible for coordinating the input of other specialists as required.

Either the tier 1 or the tier 2 resource, depending on who last worked on the task, should be responsible for tracking and closing the record of the incident even if they do not themselves resolve it. This is important as the job of incident management involves knowing when the incident has been fixed and understanding what the resolution was so this action can be tried again in the future. This is done by adding it to a Knowledge Base, which is a system that records incident resolution actions and is maintained by the service desk. The Knowledge Base can be accessed by anyone working on the service desk and some ITSM tools can automatically suggest a resolution action based on the information it sees being recorded during an incident.

At this point we need to understand the difference between the management of an incident, a problem, a service request and an access request. They are all procedurally bound activities, supported by tools with automated workflow capability, but involve different activities.

The first distinction to make is between incidents and problems. Many non-IT people class incidents as problems, which might cause issues as standard definitions are used to determine which process should be used to handle them, and, if the wrong process is used, the intended result is unlikely to be achieved. This is where the use of standard terminology is important, and it is one of the responsibilities of a service desk to make sure that people use the right terms, as the rest of the

IT department will have a specific understanding of what they mean even if the caller does not.

This responsibility can also extend to encompass users, as most service desk operations come into being through a business transformation project of some type. An example of this from my recent work concerns terminology. I had to ensure that users of a large service desk changed their description of a service-affecting issue from Problem to Incident as the service desk were all being ITIL trained and so used the correct terminology. There was no understanding from the business of what the IT definition of a problem was and this was confusing the new service desk team and led to the wrong response on occasions.

An incident is defined as the unplanned interruption to an IT service or reduction in the quality of an IT service. Failure of something that has not yet affected service, but is likely to if not dealt with, is also classed as an incident. An example of something that has not yet affected service, but might, is the failover of a system to a backup server such that a further fault will then cause an outage. This type of event frequently causes incident tickets to be raised in advance of an issue that may eventually cause a large-scale failure. An interruption to service may also be classed as a major incident if it results in significant disruption to the business or to groups of users.

A problem is defined as the cause of one or more incidents. The cause at the time the record is created is usually not known and so needs investigating. A problem is therefore one stage removed from the incident that triggers it.

Problem management is not normally within the domain of a service desk and the role responsible for this is outlined in Chapter 3, Interfaces and Dependencies; a companion book to this one will focus specifically on problem management.

However, the incident management process needs a formal interface to the problem management process as it provides the data needed to permit effective problem analysis. We should not class incidents, whether they are reported by a customer or arising from automated management tools, as problems regardless of how frequently they occur – the focus of SDIM resources should be to restore service as quickly as possible, even if it is a repeating issue.

The service desk manager should keep track of the incident volumes and types that constitute the workload of their team and be aware of the creation of problem tickets as part of the wider IT services team liaison. As the effective resolution of problem tickets will help to lower the amount of work their people have to do, a good relationship with the problem manager is important. The service desk team will also need to agree workarounds should incidents require one – this is to ensure the service is restored as quickly as possible, even if it involves a compromise. In this case, the workaround is listed and may lead to a change request for an enhancement.

Another key distinction to make is between an incident and a major incident, which is why these tasks were separated out in the job accountability in Table 2.3. All organisations will experience a significant outage at some stage that demands a different response from IT management, usually – but not always – reported via the service desk. However, it is important to note that a major incident is the highest **category** of impact for an incident and is not something different – another notion that many organisations mistakenly have. A major incident may be called a category 1 issue, or even a disaster, but it should still be recorded and handled as an incident in terms of how it is approached. However, it is often the case that such an incident is not managed by tier 1 or tier 2 staff on the service desk but by a separate, dedicated resource. This resource can either be a service manager, relationship manager or operational team leader depending on the nature of the incident, leaving the service desk to handle enquiries from other users as to what may have happened and when it is anticipated that service will resume.

The people assigned to the major incident will operate the incident management process and use the service desk management system and tools as required to keep the records updated and to restore service as quickly as possible, exactly as if it only affected one user. However, as a major incident involves a major loss of service, it will take precedence over other activities should there be a need to prioritise the response from support teams. The main reason for using a dedicated resource is that the reporting to and updating of customers, staff and others that may be affected is usually more onerous and frequent than a standard service incident. By way of example, several major UK retailers operate a major incident process as a matter of course for incidents that affect overnight store replenishment or the operation of checkout lanes at peak times, but these are still notified through the service desk as all service-facing staff need to know about them.

Extracts from job descriptions for incident management, meaning tier 1 and tier 2 personnel on the service desk, will appear in later chapters of this book as a way of showing that the SDIM role is shared by everyone who works on a service desk. In some cases, this can be dozens or even hundreds of people, which is why the use of common terminology, processes and standardised working practices is so important. There is not a standard job description for a major incident manager as the role is not one that exists in isolation. Rather, they would be someone who acts in a more senior capacity within the roles defined for service desk personnel – albeit they can have different reporting lines. During a disaster, the major incident manager may be a department head or even an IT director, especially where external services such as a customer-facing website or bank ATM network is involved – or the data centre goes down. As they have skills and authority above that of someone working on a service desk, they may need to invoke these in addition to working with the standard incident procedures.

The other activity that service desk staff frequently work on are service requests, usually regarded by users and staff alike as a positive activity that can be dealt with by either tiers 1 or 2 as appropriate. This activity is also sometimes known as request fulfilment and involves dealing with non-service-affecting tasks like a password change or providing something that involves cost and effort. Managing the commodity portfolio – the list of things that can be provided from a predefined catalogue – is different from sorting out incidents and is an important part of a service desk proposition.

The workflow and procedures used for this activity are not the same as resolving incidents and usually involve a degree of discretion, as the ability to agree such requests depends on who makes them. So, for instance, agreeing a request for a copy of Microsoft Project to be delivered to a user who has not previously had it will depend on whether they now have a job that requires it. If there is a cost involved in satisfying this request, then the service desk will need to be able to book the cost of, in this example, an extra licence to either the user's cost centre or a central IT budget, depending on the financial policy of the organisation – similarly for a new mobile phone or a set of laser printer cartridges.

If the number of service requests is low, they can be merged into the general workload although they should always be recorded separately in order to track value-added activity. If the number is large in relation to reported incidents, then the service desk may need to nominate named resources to deal with them, but note that the responsibility for doing this should always sit with the service desk even if fulfilment is assigned elsewhere. If the request involves new hardware or software, the process workflow needs to ensure that the new assets are properly recorded and accounted for in both the financial record and the configuration management information system (CMIS) that shows what assets are where and how they are connected together to form an information service.

Access requests are the other type of work that is commonly encountered by tier 1 staff. Someone may need to use an application they have not previously been authorised to use; for example, if they have been brought in to cover a colleague who is off sick and so need temporary access to a different user profile. This type of request is very easy to fulfil, although there will sometimes need to be a referral to an authorising manager to verify that the person has been assigned to do what they claim they are working on. Such requests are usually time bound and should be revoked once the time limit has been reached.

3 DEVELOPING THE ROLES AND RESPONSIBILITIES

PURPOSE AND OBJECTIVES OF JOBS WORKING ON A SERVICE DESK

The job of a service desk manager is to manage the single point of contact between a service provider and the users of their IT services, mainly, but not exclusively, in order to restore a faulty service as quickly as possible. This is achieved by the establishment of a service desk that provides call handling and management of incidents, request fulfilment and access management requests for all live services in line with agreed service level agreements (SLAs). The service desk may not be visible to the customer base, for instance if it is in a remote location to the users, or if it is distributed across several different locations. It can consist solely of employees of the service provider or a mix of employed and third-party staff or it can be completely outsourced. It is important to understand that the way it is resourced does not change its purpose; a definition is provided in the box 'service desk'.

> **Service desk:** The processing and coordination of appropriate and timely responses to incident reports, including channelling requests for help to appropriate functions for resolution, monitoring resolution activity and keeping clients appraised of progress towards service restoration.

There are five levels of job that work in a service desk function, of which the manager is one. The other roles that will be needed are supervisors, tier 2 resources, tier 1 resources and administration support or trainees. Figure 3.1 shows a typical hierarchy of jobs that exist at these five levels.

Figure 3.1 The hierarchy of jobs working on a service desk

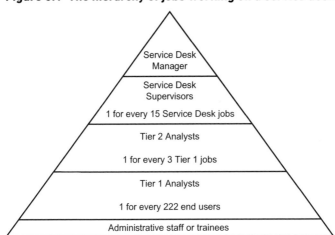

This pyramid representation is based on the usual management rule that the most senior job is at the top and the most junior is at the bottom. However, in customer service terms, the people working directly to support users are those in the middle – akin to the filling in a sandwich. The jobs of management, supervision and administration exist to ensure that the service objectives are met by the people at tiers 1 and 2 and it can be seen from this roughly how many people are needed at each level. These ratios, like any management ratio, are not prescriptive but have been derived from dozens of assignments on service desks in a wide variety of industries and are a useful guide. For instance, consider a service desk supporting 10,000 busy users in a single organisation. Based on the guidelines in Figure 3.1, this could translate to a function needing the following numbers of people:

Job	Number	Rationale
Service desk manager	1	Only one job is needed
Service desk supervisor	4	Based on 1 to every 15 people
Tier 2 analyst	15	A ratio of 1 to every 3 tier 1 staff handling the more complex issues
Tier 1 analyst	45	A ratio of 10,000 to 222 for a function operating over a 12-hour day
Administrative support	2	Not based on a ratio but on the amount of housekeeping work required. This can be higher if the people doing this job are also being trained for tier 1 work or lower if clerical support comes from a shared pool managed elsewhere

These numbers of people would be needed to manage a service desk over a 12-hour day, six days a week, working to prescribed standards of performance and challenging SLAs across a few hundred different applications.

Some organisations only staff the desk during office hours, whilst others provide round-the-clock support and this will influence the number of people needed on duty at any point.

One of the tasks usually done by the administrative support resource is to track the number of incidents by hour of day and day of week and construct a staffing rota in 15- or 30-minute increments. This is then used to match the number of people available to manage incidents and service requests to the expected volume that may be encountered based on recent history. Another important clerical task is to analyse and publish the performance figures that will be shown to both the service desk and user population. Whilst it is not always the case that a pipeline of staff is needed to take on jobs at tier 1 and tier 2, a prudent manager will always be looking at their staff turnover figures to ensure that enough people are likely to be available to work on the desk. This is often how a clerical resource can be fast-tracked into a job, providing they want to work at a higher level, as they will be familiar with how their colleagues behave and the nature of the work that they do.

There is an implicit assumption that contact with the service desk can only be made by telephone. However, this is not how every customer in today's world chooses to access service, and the mechanisms used by modern service desks will encompass telephone, email and self-logging via a portal, live chat and walk-up mechanisms as required depending on location, customer preference and the way that services are segmented. It is important to establish the most appropriate service ethos to match company preferences.

For example, a very popular service desk deployment at a leading London law firm had a central team in IT dealing with phone and self-service queries, with satellites placed on each floor to deal with walk-up queries. They all used the same incident management and reporting systems, but the way they interacted with their customers was adjusted to meet their needs. This was regarded by the lawyers as extremely supportive as they could access personal help without having to go through telephone menus. Many universities adopt the same approach by offering a 'walk in' service to support students, particularly during freshers' week or before final exams when the need for an immediate and personal response is especially critical.

The job of people working at tiers 1 and 2 is to perform one or more of the roles within a service desk. Whilst the obvious one will be to log incidents, attempt first line resolution and manage any escalation and closure as required, most service desk staff will rotate around all three tasks of incident management, access management and request fulfilment in order to provide variety and to increase their skills, knowledge and understanding of customer needs.

The coordination and control of the work of incident management falls to supervisors and the service desk manager in a typical chain of command as outlined in Figure 3.1. Whilst the actions to manage incidents will be undertaken at tiers 1 and 2, the work to resolve the technical reasons causing them may lie with technical specialists outside the service desk; how they are controlled is addressed in the section Interfaces and Dependencies on page 52.

The tasks of SDIM are important because the dialogue between a service provider and its customers has to be managed in a consistent and timely fashion. Before these roles existed, technical resources had to deal with both their core work and direct interactions with customers whenever something went wrong, which is inefficient in terms of time and meant they were diverted from their task.

A good way of summarising the objectives of a service desk manager is as shown in Figure 3.2, which is taken from a recent, real-life job description.

Figure 3.2 Incident management responsibilities of a service desk manager

Ensures that all incidents, requests for assistance and provision of commodity items (including access management) are handled effectively across all channels within agreed KPIs, to meet agreed Service Levels and to deliver Customer Satisfaction.

An important terminology point is made here in respect of job titles. Whilst that of a service desk manager is ubiquitous and rarely varies between different organisations, the job titles given to staff on a service desk differ widely. They are variously called incident manager, service analyst, service desk engineer, support analyst or even service delivery specialist. The job title is not important, but the role they play and the accountabilities they hold are what define their job and we will use all the titles interchangeably. What you, the reader, only need to remember is that they are all SDIM jobs.

SKILLS

The skills needed to perform the roles both of management and dealing with incidents are very varied. There is no unique training path for staff working in SDIM and they do not necessarily even need to have an IT background – it is service orientation and customer empathy which matters most as technical and management skills can be acquired more easily than the others can. However, the majority of staff in these jobs will be on a career path in IT, which means they will look to progress both within their function and to other jobs depending on their age, inclination and the availability of related roles. The section Interfaces and Dependencies will look at the related and interdependent roles that service desk staff will engage with, and where they may look to in terms of career progression.

There is, as in all jobs, a skills hierarchy and, as already described, there are five job levels with well-defined skills profiles for all of them. A basic example of an incident management skill is summarised in this statement:

'Has good oral communication skills and can take an analytical approach to solving issues. Possesses a basic knowledge of IT and knowledge of several generic desktop software tools and, where applicable, deeper knowledge of at least one of the software applications used within their organisation.'

This summary statement clearly needs to be expanded for each of the five job levels that do the work of SDIM. These are generally known as trainees (or clerical support), tier 1 and tier 2 staff, supervisors and management in ascending order of responsibility. An expanded statement can be much more specific about what the job entails and what skills will be needed to do it properly. Figure 3.3 is taken from the job description of an incident manager working at tier 2. This job existed as part of a team of 50 people.

Figure 3.3 The skills needed by an incident manager working at tier 2

- Has a working knowledge of the services provided by IT and the landscape of the underpinning processes and IT infrastructure (hardware, databases, operating systems, local area networks, etc.).

- Has well developed interpersonal skills critical to the establishment of relationships at the initial point of contact.

- Is able to communicate effectively orally, in writing and via emails.

- Has good analytical skills and can acquire a proper understanding of a problem or situation by breaking it down systematically into its component parts, identifying the relationships between these parts, identifying gaps in the available information and devising means of remedying such gaps selecting the appropriate method/tool to resolve the problem and reflecting on the result.

- Demonstrates an understanding of Customer Value Chain concepts including the complete sequence of activities within a process from receipt of an order or request to delivery of a product or service.

(Continued)

Figure 3.3 (Continued)

- Is familiar with techniques for ensuring that full account is taken of customers' real and stated needs in the delivery of IT services.

- Demonstrates an understanding of the structures and activities of all departments for which services are provided.

- Demonstrates an understanding of the purpose and composition of Service Level Agreements and the relationship between an SLA, OLA and a contract for supply of services.

- Demonstrates an awareness of ITIL processes and how they impact on the role of the service desk, specifically Incident Management, Problem Management, Change Management and Request Fulfilment.

- Demonstrates up-to-date knowledge of the Operational and Service Architecture; IT infrastructure (hardware, databases, operating systems, local area networks, etc.) and the IT applications and service processes used within the organisation.

- Tier 2 support analysts will have a minimum of two areas of extra technical depth over the tier 1 analysts and over time this skill depth should cover all areas.

- Will generally be skilled in user admin facilities across the complete range of systems and technologies and be able to complete even the most complex requests.

- Is aware of the principles, methods and techniques for documenting standards such as programming standards, quality standards, health and safety standards, etc.

(Continued)

Figure 3.3 (Continued)

> • Is familiar with configuration management, the
> discipline which gives precise control over IT assets
> by allowing IT management to maintain information
> about the 'configuration items', including hardware
> devices, computer programs, documentation,
> telecommunications services and computer centre
> facilities, required to deliver an IT service.

This is clearly a very comprehensive list of skills, which is why a tier 2 position will typically be well regarded and rewarded as a key IT job.

The way in which incident management jobs are designed varies from organisation to organisation and so it is useful to have a common frame of reference within which to place each job. The most practical reference is SFIA and Table 3.1 is an extract from the SFIA framework showing the five levels from an entry job at Level 1 to the overall manager's job at Level 5.

Table 3.1 The service desk skills hierarchy within SFIA

Category	Service Management Skills	Code	Level						
			1	2	3	4	5	6	7
Service operation	Service desk & incident management	USUP	1	2	3	4	5		

Reproduced by kind permission of the SFIA Foundation.

It is appropriate at this point to understand a little more about the characteristics of the levels within SFIA, without going into great detail for the whole IT organisation, so that we can understand how the hierarchy works. SFIA skill levels are generic in that anyone at, say, Level 4 in one discipline will have the same types of accountabilities and responsibilities as someone in another discipline even though their underlying skill types will be different. This is important when selecting staff for particular roles as they will need both the **level** characteristics and the **technical** prerequisites of the skill in order to be able to do the job to an appropriate standard. Let us look at an example of the seven skill levels of SFIA, as shown in Figure 3.4.

Figure 3.4 SFIA skills definitions by level

Level 1	Follow
Level 2	Assist
Level 3	Apply
Level 4	Enable
Level 5	Ensure; advise
Level 6	Initiate; influence
Level 7	Set strategy; inspire; mobilise

The words associated with each level exist to characterise the type of activity each level requires in order to satisfy the objectives for it. Each level also has four generic dimensions that need to be demonstrated before someone performing at that level can be regarded as working appropriately.

These generic dimensions are:

- autonomy;
- influence;

- complexity;
- business skills.

Each job is assessed against these four dimensions, which can then be used to define what the job holder is able to do and what training they need in order to do their job. So, for example, the dimensions for Level 1 are shown in Table 3.2.

Table 3.2 SFIA skills dimensions for Level 1 – a trainee or admin post

Level 1	Follow
Autonomy	Works under close supervision. Uses little discretion. Expected to seek guidance in unexpected situations.
Influence Complexity	Interacts with department. Performs routine activities in a structured environment. Requires assistance in resolving unexpected problems.
Business skills	Uses basic IS functions, applications and processes. Demonstrates an organised approach to work. Capable of learning new skills and applying acquired knowledge. Basic oral and written communication skills. Contributes to identifying own development opportunities.

Compare this with the same dimensions described for a Level 5 post in Table 3.3.

Table 3.3 SFIA skills dimensions for Level 5 – a typical service desk manager job

Level 5	Ensure, advise
Autonomy	Works under broad direction. Work is often self-initiated. Is fully accountable for meeting allocated technical and/or project/supervisory objectives. Establishes milestones and has a significant role in the delegation of responsibilities.
Influence	Influences organisation, customers, suppliers, partners and peers on the contribution of own specialism. Builds appropriate and effective business relationships. Makes decisions which impact the success of assigned projects i.e. results, deadlines and budget. Has significant influence over the allocation and management of resources appropriate to given assignments.
Complexity	Performs an extensive range and variety of complex technical and/or professional work activities. Undertakes work which requires the application of fundamental principles in a wide and often unpredictable range of contexts. Understands the relationship between own specialism and wider customer needs.

(Continued)

Table 3.3 (Continued)

Level 5	Ensure, advise
Business skills	Advises on the available standards, methods, tools and applications relevant to own specialism and can make appropriate choices from alternatives. Analyses, designs, plans, executes and evaluates work to time, cost and quality targets. Assesses and evaluates risk. Communicates effectively, both formally and informally. Demonstrates leadership. Facilitates collaboration between stakeholders who have diverse objectives. Understands the relevance of own area of responsibility/specialism to the employing organisation. Takes initiatives to keep skills up to date.

This shows that, within the same four dimensions, there is a hierarchy of responsibilities with a clear understanding of what needs to be done in each dimension to satisfy the requirements. As we know, service desk staff can work across all four of these dimensions but not all the characteristics are reproduced here as this would be a distraction. Also, the business skills dimensions for Level 5 shown in Table 3.3 have been truncated in the interests of clarity, whereas the SFIA framework contains more detail.

This hierarchy is significant in that SFIA 5 is a management level that can qualify someone working at this level, for at least three of the past five years, for Chartered IT Professional (CITP) status, a key measure of professionalism. It can be seen that Level 5 is appropriate to someone running a sizeable service desk, or perhaps acting as a major incident manager; people working in these jobs are generally regarded as senior IT professionals.

By reference to the preceding tables and framework, the typical accountabilities for a tier 1 incident manager will exist at SFIA Level 2 – not the lowest skill level available. This often surprises organisations when they are carrying out an organisation design as they usually look to provide resources at the least possible cost rather than the highest possible value. This is a big mistake, as work performed by the service desk is critical to the reputation of the IT department, and staff working on it need both the skills and organisational recognition to be able to discharge this – the accountabilities of dealing with users who have lost service are extremely important ones and all staff need the skills to be able to do this effectively. So, someone working at tier 1 will be expected to work to the job purpose described in Figure 3.5.

Figure 3.5 The skills needed by an analyst working at tier 1

Following agreed Service Desk procedures, provides tier 1 support to users on services which are available to them and underpinning systems, products and services across all commodity services, user account, email and Shared Drive administration. Includes VIP and critical incident management.

Operates and administers logical access controls and directly associated security services relating to all platforms used in order to provide continuous and secure access to information services.

Note that VIP (very important person) and critical (another term for major) incident management exists in the skills requirement even at tier 1. This is because the purpose of, say, an inbound call is unlikely to be known in advance and so whoever deals with it may have to interact with a senior executive (or someone calling on their behalf) and to understand that a major outage is more significant than a single user issue. It is possible that the call could be referred to someone else, but this is not necessarily required as handling a service issue for a VIP user is no different from any other – the service management tool used to handle incidents can be implemented with workflows to allow an incident to be routed through a different SLA path. This is because a service failure immediately before the completion of a large merger proposal will be of higher importance than a single PC problem in the post room and so needs fixing more quickly. This is what persuaded the London law firm mentioned in a previous example to place support personnel near the offices of senior partners in order to deliver service instantly rather than over the phone.

Other types of functions that are also carried out by a service desk include:

- training: to address 'how do I?' queries as a service value-add feature, as opposed to just logging every call as an incident or access request;
- multilingual support: to address customer requests from different countries or where there are multiple languages within one company;
- usability support: to ensure that staff with special needs or disabilities can be accommodated from an IT support perspective;
- FOI (Freedom of Information Act) queries: specifically for public sector organisations where such requests need to be formally logged;
- support for the introduction of new projects into live working: with an especial focus on the supportability and escalation procedures.

It would be unusual to have to provide staff with all these skills on a general service desk, and other specialists, typically technical support personnel, could be an appropriate point of referral once the initial request has been taken and assessed. However, it is common to find staff at tier 2 being able to offer practical advice on, say, a spreadsheet query, and for people who are proficient in more than one language to work at both tiers 1 and 2 where the job requires them to interact with users in other countries.

We will look at some typical salaries for all frontline job levels in Chapter 5. However, these are very variable according to company type and geographic location and so should not be taken as anything more than a general guide.

RESPONSIBILITIES

Whilst it is tempting to publish a full set of job descriptions for all five job levels in this section, this would be counterproductive as each organisation interprets the needs of their customers in different ways – especially if they are external to the organisation rather than being company employees. This is because the role of an analyst supporting many different businesses is often either more constrained, as they only handle one type of incident, or more diverse, in that they can also offer new services. So we will offer a number of real-life examples for you to use as case studies rather than prescriptive templates, which in reality cannot exist.

What is provided here are a number of ideas that have been proven to work in high-performing organisations in every industry sector. What is important to note is the task breakdown in terms of time allocation by different types of responsibility owned by the different service desk jobs. Again, this is not prescriptive, but indicates how to approach job design for the different roles that exist in the world of service desk management. We will look at four SDIM jobs in this section – that of a service desk manager, a team leader or supervisor, a tier 2 analyst and a tier 1 analyst – as these are the most representative roles in the incident management hierarchy. Figure 3.6 shows how the workload of a service desk manager can be typified in terms of the time that needs to be spent on various tasks.

Figure 3.6 The breakdown of responsibilities for a service desk manager

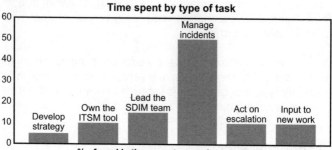

% of weekly time spent on each type of task

This complements the initial summary in Table 2.3 of Chapter 2, and the detail behind this can be amplified by reference to a real SDIM example. What follows in the next six tables, Tables 3.4 to 3.9, is a full task breakdown of the work of a service desk manager of a large organisation supporting over 20,000 users, showing what tasks make up the working week as described in Figure 3.6.

Table 3.4 Tasks involved in developing an SDIM strategy and function

Responsibilities	Key tasks	% of time spent
Develops and implements the strategy, standards and procedures	• Create the Service Desk strategy. • Develop, own and maintain the Incident Management process.	5%

(Continued)

Table 3.4 (Continued)

Responsibilities	Key tasks	% of time spent
within which the IT Service Desk will operate.	• Develop, own and maintain the Major Incident process. • Develop, gain agreement to and maintain the escalation procedures. • Develop and manage the KPIs. • Create the framework for the documentation of standards and ensure adherence. • Operate the Access Management process as defined by ISM. • Develop and maintain the Service Request process. • Develop and own Customer Service standards against which all Service Desk personnel will be measured. • Manage the Knowledge Base and ensure that support documentation is developed for business applications and for the Service Desk personnel to enable users and staff to do their respective jobs.	

Table 3.5 Tasks involved in defining and maintaining an ITSM toolset

Responsibilities	Key tasks	% of time spent
Owns the Service Desk tool and ensures that it continues to meet functional requirements.	• Define the requirements for the Service Desk. • Ensure through the technical support area that the Service Desk is maintained to meet the required standards of service. • Ensure that the Service Desk tool (ITSM) remains fit for purpose. • Define and agree future developments for the Service Desk tool.	10%

Table 3.6 Tasks involved in leading and managing the SDIM team

Responsibilities	Key tasks	% of time spent
Provides team leadership and management for the Service Desk team so that they are skilled and motivated to carry out their roles.	• Carry out the Performance Management process for all staff in the team. • Identify the development needs for all staff within the Service Desk and maintain a Training and Development plan which meets the needs of the services provided, and the individuals, to meet demand. • Provide on-the-job coaching as appropriate. • Obtain qualitative customer feedback on the Service Desk Performance.	15%

Table 3.7 Tasks involved in delivering incident and request management

Responsibilities	Key tasks	% of time spent
Ensures that all incidents and requests for assistance and commodity items (including access management) are handled effectively across all channels within agreed KPIs, to meet agreed service levels and to deliver customer satisfaction.	• Ensure that the catalogue of services underpinned by the inventory of components is complete and up to date. • Plan resources to meet demand. • Monitor the performance of the Service Desk through the development of KPIs and report against them on a monthly basis. • Work closely with resolving areas and other Service Desk personnel to ensure continuity of services. • Review service level information and the contribution made by the Service Desk. • Obtain customer feedback to evaluate the level of customer satisfaction delivered by the Service Desk.	50%

(Continued)

Table 3.7 (Continued)

Responsibilities	Key tasks	% of time spent
	• Investigate system access enquiries referred by support staff and, in conjunction with ISM, implement and adopt known techniques to satisfy new access requirements, or provide an effective interface between users and service providers when existing facilities are considered inadequate.	

Table 3.8 Tasks involved when acting on escalation

Responsibilities	Key tasks	% of time spent
Provides an effective interface on escalation between users and service providers where requests cannot be resolved satisfactorily or where incidents are of a highly critical or sensitive nature to preserve and enhance customer relations.	• Act as the point of escalation for issues raised by analysts or users and provide arbitration where necessary. • Manage high-profile critical or complex incidents as required and provide updates to Customer Relationship Management and users where necessary. • Influence cross-functional teams to enable successful solutions.	10%

Table 3.9 Tasks involved when working to bring new projects into service

Responsibilities	Key tasks	% of time spent
Provides input to projects where new services are being developed and deploys resources for BAU testing on commodity services as part of the development and change processes respectively.	• Ensure that the project takes account of contextual factors in the definition of functional and non-functional requirements and in the developing design. • Identify, in conjunction with IT project managers, the demand for BAU testing as required by the changes to existing commodity services. • Identify, in conjunction with IT project managers, the requirement for Service Desk input to project work and the requirements definitions for service support and documentation for potential new services. • Interpret requirements from changes to service or new services and develop support documentation for non-technical users and the Service Desk analysts.	10%

(Continued)

Table 3.9 (Continued)

Responsibilities	Key tasks	% of time spent
	• Analyse the impact of new services on the Service Desk and develop solutions as appropriate to provide service including resourcing, hours of service, development of the Knowledge Base, etc.	

The responsibility allocation matches the expectations of the skill level that such a job needs, and the anticipated time allocation shown is based on what a typical organisation with a high project workload, say 10–20 new implementations each quarter, would require. It is also based on the fact that staff turnover in incident management is usually higher than other areas of IT – up to 25 per cent per annum in some cases - as a result partly of working in a pressured environment but also as the junior levels are seen as ones to get in order to move into another IT job. This requires a significant degree of team leadership and performance management from the service desk manager and is why, in this example, the allocation of 15 per cent of each week was needed to recruit, train, motivate and evaluate their staff.

The responsibility breakdowns for the other three job levels we will look at are not set out in the same detail in order to simplify the presentation. Instead, the main areas of activity, with the time spent on each, are shown in Table 3.10. As an administrative post may also work for other functions as well as on the service desk, it has not been included in this table.

Table 3.10 A high-level breakdown of responsibilities for other service desk roles

Role	Responsibility	% of time spent
Team leader	Supervision of the team	30%
	Workload scheduling for the team	20%
	Incident management on escalation or by intervention	20%
	Review access management requests for violations	10%
	Assist users in 'how to' queries	10%
	Provide input to project teams	10%
Tier 2 analyst	Handle incidents and requests referred from tier 1	80%
	Create and maintain support documents for service desk and others	10%
	Release testing for service items within the commodity portfolio	10%
Tier 1 analyst	Handle incidents and service requests	80%
	Reset passwords and grant access requests in line with ISM policies	20%

Not surprisingly, the time to task demands for a tier 1 analyst are more heavily skewed towards direct incident management and request fulfilment than are the other jobs. In contrast, tier 2 analysts are available to handle more complex customer calls on escalation as well as being responsible for some offline tasks, such as creating and maintaining support documentation, which, when working with a modern ITSM tool, will mean updating its Knowledge Base. This additional responsibility should also involve a degree of *ad hoc* customer support in addition to handling incidents since the resolution achieved, based on a good understanding of the issue, is what will be added to the Knowledge Base.

As might be expected, supervisors are mainly responsible for planning the rotas for their staff as well as ensuring that their teams maintain performance and good customer relationships – especially in the case of a major incident. It will normally be the role of a supervisor to decide if an automated response is needed to alert customers through the call handling system (ACD), service desk portal and/or intranet bulletin boards in the event of a major incident happening. The advantages of providing a pre-recorded message or a script on the intranet system are that consistent information can be offered to people who experience difficulties and try and make contact; that the amount of repetition that service desk staff experience can be limited; and that other, unrelated incidents can be reported without major congestion. Whilst good planning and service orientation across IT will limit the potential for major incidents, the service desk should always be prepared for one to happen and have the mechanisms available to respond quickly. Again, this is part of fulfilling the remit as outlined at the start of this chapter.

INTERFACES AND DEPENDENCIES

None of the roles described exist in isolation; rather they are part of the overall IT department and so work within it rather than autonomously. The service desk cannot resolve every incident themselves – this sometimes has to be the role of others. So, whilst the SDIM team will remain in control of customer liaison, they depend on the rest of IT to provide updates on the resolution of incidents that may have been delegated to them.

Which other functions are most engaged with the SDIM function? In incident process terms, this is easy to answer:

- Specialist support teams, for issues affecting systems or infrastructure.
- Problem management, for the investigation of any underlying causes.
- Information security management, for access policies and delegation.
- Service level management, for issues affecting published SLAs.
- External providers and subcontractors in the service chain.

Specialist support teams act as the resolver groups to which incidents affecting, say, a sales reporting system or a network will be referred in the event that an initial triage on the service desk indicates that the incident cannot be managed at tiers 1 or 2 or requires deeper technical input. The SDIM person handling the incident will decide that they cannot resolve it themselves and so will refer it out using the tools that will have been provided to them. It is good practice for these specialist resolver groups to be linked to the service desk workflow so that incidents and their assigned priority levels are presented in the context of the reported issue – merely alerting them of an issue by email is not usually an appropriate mechanism.

It is possible that, in the case of a team of five or six people, the referral will be sent to a queue that everyone can see, or perhaps it may instead be routed to a team leader who looks after issues that involve different time zones. Once the incident has been referred out, the OLA (operational level agreement) clock will be started and the service desk management system will keep track of the time remaining and alert SDIM or resolver group management accordingly when there has been or is likely to be an SLA breach. The specialist support team to which the incident has been referred is responsible for determining what resolution is required and documenting that resolution, in the incident record that is passed back to

SDIM, for verification with the user who reported it so it can then be closed. The service desk manager will act as the point of escalation for incidents causing an SLA breach and will react accordingly – the service level manager will need to be informed of repeated breaches, but not always in real time.

Problem management as an activity is important but is not always carried out by a formally constituted team. Companies allocate problem-management responsibilities in different ways, depending on what is perceived to be the underlying issue, so the SDIM team may need to work with different individuals each time. The problem-management process itself, however, is essential in anything other than the smallest IT department as it is responsible (as we saw in the second section of Chapter 2) for the investigation of the underlying cause of one or more incidents. If there is an incident that has not been fully cleared, even though service has been restored by means of a workaround, this information will need to be passed on by the SDIM team for further analysis and investigation as it will help with any subsequent work to understand the root cause.

It may be that, in the case of a systems issue in a company that does not have a dedicated problem management function, the problem request may be routed to the application support team. This is not the same as resolving an incident, however, and the service desk escalation mechanism needs to make this clear. The same will go for any technical resolving area such as network support or database administration. Problem management may not always be regarded as a priority for resolver groups, which is why it is better to separate it out entirely.

Information security management (ISM) is the function responsible for creating and owning an organisation's security policies. It can devolve day-to-day control of work such as password resets and access control requests to non-sensitive applications, and similar activity, to the service desk. This will clearly need to be done on the basis that the access control framework is sufficiently rigorous to allow this to take place without compromising confidentiality. The major advantage of

working in this way is to fulfil the remit of the se
being the primary point of liaison with customers, an
such requests will allow ISM to work on more strategic i

One of the tasks of a service desk supervisor is to alert IS
to inappropriate or unusual requests, so the relationship can
work well for both parties – especially when the service desk
operates outside the hours that the ISM function is available,
such as at weekends. The exercise of delegated authority to
grant people access to facilities and applications they may not
have previously used – such as for a locum in a pharmacy or
temporary workers hired in just to cover seasonal activity over
Christmas – does not require ISM skills.

An example of this concerns my own experience when
introducing a new internet security policy for the organisation
I worked at in the 1990s. Part of my job was to talk to all
the senior management groups in the company about how
important it was to set the internet filters at a level that
allowed them to do their jobs whilst preventing inappropriate
material from being accessed. I assembled some examples of
such material in preparation for these talks and requested a
software package in order to display it properly. This request
alerted a service desk supervisor once the content type
became apparent and I needed an adult conversation about
why I had such stuff on my laptop. It was a relief to him that
the material was appropriate for the purpose and that it would
all be deleted immediately after presentation.

The interface with **service level management** is an interesting
one. SLM is mainly concerned with the creation of a service
catalogue, which is either a system or other structured form
of recording information about live IT services including points
of contact, pricing and other details that is then published to
customers. SLM is also responsible for the identification of
service level requirements, such as transaction throughput
or response times, and for negotiating SLAs with customers.
The service catalogue and the resulting SLAs are then used by
the service desk teams to set priorities and assign actions to the
appropriate resolver groups based on an understanding of what
agreements are in place with each customer or group of users.

proves impossible to meet when
…d type of incidents being recorded,
…r needs to alert the service level
…the SLA needs to be renegotiated.
…t interaction as the result may be
…in resolver groups, or within SDIM
…class of service being offered and
…r the system redesigned. If there
…level manager, then the service
…esk manager needs to refer SLA issues to whoever in the organisation exercises that responsibility. This interplay between SDIM and SLM is important as the service desk will be penalised in customer surveys if they are perceived to be underachieving against expectations set by the published service catalogue.

It is rare to find that an in-house IT function is responsible for every aspect of service delivery – there is usually a range of **external providers and subcontractors** who are responsible for specific, and sometimes significant, elements of the overall IT service. This can range from outsourced network providers and cloud-sourced backup arrangements through to desktop support and offshore application support – all of which will be bound by SLAs and commercial contracts of some sort. These external suppliers need to be engaged in the same way as an in-house team, based on whatever contract is in place – whilst an internal team will work to some form of agreement, like an OLA, external suppliers will have more formal SLAs with associated contractual penalties for underperformance.

It is vital that the service desk routes incident reports to external suppliers as quickly as possible following triage as they may be operating in a different country or a different time zone. This escalation is the same as for an in-house team and their response would be monitored in a very similar way, but this will depend on whether the supplier is directly contracted or indirectly contracted. Figure 3.7 illustrates an example of the chain of accountability that exists when either all or part of an IT activity is contracted out to specialist companies.

Figure 3.7 Example of an accountability chain for contracted services

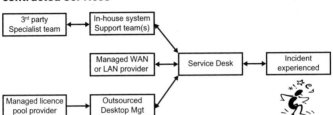

If a third-party supplier is responsible for delivering part of a service, as shown in Figure 3.7, they will be managed through the service desk in the same way as any other resolver group would be. This may involve an electronic connection between the service desk of the customer and the service infrastructure of the supplier. This adds to the complexity of the ITSM tool and its workflow, but, however this is achieved, it should be seamless to the business customer. This responsibility is normally best managed by listing such agreements in the service catalogue and detailing the times when it is appropriate to engage directly and when the linkage has to be through the in-house resource, depending on how the contract has been structured. Holding contracted SLAs in the ITSM tool is generally regarded as best practice where the tool itself provides such capability.

Managing incident flows between an in-house service desk and, say, three different offshore application service providers, as well as several different infrastructure providers, is no small matter, as anyone working in a modern, cloud-sourced organisation will understand. It is, however, absolutely essential in order to preserve the responsibility of the service desk as the primary point of liaison. In the example given in Figure 3.7, the service desk acts as the incident owner, delegating an action to one resolver group as a task, which means that, whilst the overall SLA clock is ticking, the resolver group is tracked within its agreed OLA. Another resolver group may well also be working on a different aspect of the same issue, not uncommon in situations where there has been something that has triggered multiple system failures, but with a different OLA expectation. The service desk retains control of the overall SLA, which is what has been agreed with the customer, throughout. In situations where the service desk faces off to external suppliers, it is expected that regular meetings will take place between the two parties to agree expectations and to review performance against KPIs. This is a key task for the service desk management team.

One important note to be aware of, however, is what actions external suppliers are contractually obliged to undertake in order to resolve any issues reported to them. Whilst it is standard practice to expect them to resolve incidents, they may not be obliged to undertake root-cause analysis and so cannot be relied upon to offer more than incremental resolution. This is especially the case where their contract rewards them on a per-fix basis for referred incidents, and in these circumstances it would not be in their commercial interest to identify underlying problems.

Equally, it is often the case that, although the contract may not stipulate payment-per-fix, the skill set of the supplier may not extend to root-cause analysis and so they would not be able to perform problem management. Both these situations are something the service desk needs to be aware of and to discuss with both the supplier and the procurement team responsible for establishing the outsourcing contract as, otherwise, incident volumes could remain at an unacceptably high and commercially damaging level.

It is sometimes the case that a service desk faces customers external to their organisation as well as internal users of IT services. The expectations of such customers can rarely be managed in the same way that internal users can – partly because there is no constant relationship with them but mainly because there may not be a contracted SLA either. An example of this could be a mobile service provider offering resolution to consumers within a set time period, but where there is no comeback if this is exceeded. The organisation may publish service level targets (SLTs) for public facing operations, but these are not the same as SLAs because the customer cannot enforce them. SLTs in these situations tend to be much broader – say, 72 hours to fix a customer broadband connection – than internal SLAs, which are usually counted in hours rather than days. The task of the service desk team managing the incident management process in these situations needs to be governed by different criteria rather than a metric such as percentage of SLAs met. The customer in these circumstances has more commercial leeway, so diplomacy and assurance that the SLT can be met will always be needed and this is where managing customer MOTs becomes important.

INTRODUCING MOMENTS OF TRUTH

MOTs happen every time a customer comes into contact with your organisation. In a transport system, this might be as short as 15 seconds per encounter between a customer and an employee, but this is still long enough for an opinion to be formed about the company that the employee represents. MOTs happen all the time and customers form either conscious or subconscious impressions of how a company operates by how each individual aspect of service is delivered. What happens as a result of cumulative MOTs is that customers make long-term decisions about who they wish to do business with based on what is often a remarkably short service exposure.

The MOT concept was first postulated by Scandinavian Airlines in the 1980s as a means of restoring the company to good health by removing everything that was not adding value to the customer experience. It was calculated that every one of their 10 million customers came into contact with five employees for 15 seconds each, an annual customer exposure of some 208,000 hours. In that time, none of those 50 million MOTs considered how well the aircraft might have been maintained, what level of capital investment the company was planning for the coming year or how well the hanger administration worked. Instead, those 208,000 hours of contact were spent assessing the quality of the 'contract' between the airline and the passenger, including how smartly the staff were dressed – and yet these issues were not discussed at board meetings, whereas the items mentioned earlier were.

The overall quality of a customer 'contract' is therefore based on the cumulative experiences a customer has based on their contact with an organisation and this is ideally suited for use within an IT service delivery department as the underlying issues are the same. Airlines and IT delivery organisations exist to provide a customer service – as an example of this, Figure 3.8 illustrates a typical customer journey as shown by the management of an IT incident from initial reception through to completion.

So it can be seen that the frontline teams carry a great deal of responsibility for the corporate image of IT as a whole. They can also be used as the ambassadors for the MOT concept in the organisation by setting themselves as role models, but only once they have successfully demonstrated good service. The reason why service desk personnel operate at the middle end of the accountability framework rather than at the bottom end is because of the cumulative customer opinion that is formed by the amount of contact with them. Service desk personnel must be empowered not only as individuals but also by the processes they use, plus the technology they interact with, to deliver service and to ensure that their colleagues do the same in line with SLAs. This means that the SDIM team, as the major point of contact with the customer, is in a good position to champion the MOT principle in the wider IT organisation.

The MOT principles can be described in four simple statements:

- Everyone needs to know and feel that they are needed.

- Everyone wants to be treated as an individual.

- Giving someone the freedom to take responsibility releases resources that would otherwise remain concealed.

- An individual without empowerment cannot take responsibility, whereas an empowered individual cannot help but take responsibility.

Figure 3.8 The customer journey as an example of the MOT potential

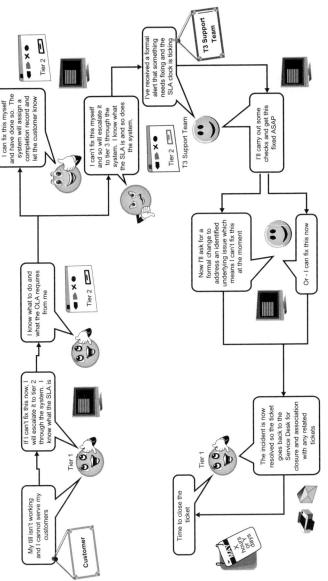

Reproduced by courtesy of Carole Ratcliffe.

If we take the example of an organisation fielding 15,000 IT service calls to its help desks per month, we can see that a big MOT potential exists. In this example, three employees were involved on each incident resolution for an average of 6 minutes 35 seconds on each occasion, a total of 59,250 hours contact time with users being experienced in a year. This level of exposure was actually far greater than the amount of time IT management believed they were exposed to customers – which was based on a simple calculation of 10 managers attending a monthly customer meeting for 2 hours a time, a total of 240 hours a year. So it can come as a surprise when a corporate decision is announced that, for instance, the IT department is being considered as a potential for being outsourced or that service quality is not – to the customer – what the IT management team understands it to be.

It is clearly rather late in the day to be faced with defending your service record when there is a mismatch between what you believe to have been a good service and what the organisation says it has received. The inputs to such decisions arise not from experiencing 'service as normal' or the 240 hours a year of what may well have been effective management contribution, but the cumulative exposure to 59,250 hours a year of incident experience, which is why the MOT concept is an important one for service delivery to embrace. This is not only important to the service desk team, but also to anyone else in IT that has a need to work directly with a user.

Customer opinions about IT are rarely driven by an SLA, but are instead based on perceptions and personal experiences. In one organisation, an annual customer survey revealed that a branch manager's opinion of the hardware maintenance company being used to support her cashiers' equipment was based solely around the personal hygiene of the engineer, not his ability to do the job or the highly competitive price at which this was achieved. This type of feedback is common and yet is rarely sought or, if it is, rarely acted upon despite the fact that such issues can be more readily, if more sensitively, addressed than something of a more systemic nature.

Many IT organisations have lost the confidence of their customers by the way in which service was delivered and not just by the cost – which can often be quite low. Outsourcing companies can often provide a service desk capability at a lower cost than an in-house function, but if the way this works over time fails the MOT test, then companies will look to bring the capability back under their direct management once more if customer feedback warrants it. This is the exact opposite of outsourcing and has been the situation in several of the organisations used as examples in this book.

More detail on the MOT concept can be found in the seminal book, *Moments of Truth*,[1] by Jan Carlzon, formerly the CEO of Scandinavian Airlines (SAS), and the techniques of deploying this in IT can be found in a companion book, *World Class IT Service Delivery*,[2] by Peter Wheatcroft, published by BCS.

---

[1] *Moments of Truth* by Jan Carlzon is published in paperback under ISBN 0-06-091580-3

[2] *World Class IT Service Delivery* by Peter Wheatcroft is published under ISBN 13 978-1-902505-82-4

4 TOOLS, METHODS AND TECHNIQUES

REFERENCES AND STANDARDS

The only internationally recognised **standard** against which the processes used for SDIM can be assessed is ISO/IEC 20000-1:2011. This is a benchmark that specifies the requirements of a service management system (SMS) to allow a service provider to plan, implement and maintain an SMS appropriate to its needs. ISO/IEC 20000-1:2011 is a development of the 2005 edition, which was itself a development of the original BS 15000 standard, which first set out the requirements that need to be met in order to gain certification for IT service management.

ISO/IEC 20000-1:2011 is used internationally and, at the time of writing, there are 40 organisations in the UK, out of a total of 733 organisations worldwide, that have current certificates in force.[1] ISO/IEC 20000-1:2011 is part of a family of related publications, which together provide the information needed to plan for certification. Currently, the ISO/IEC 20000 series consists of:

Part 1: Service management system (SMS) requirements. This is the standard itself, which an auditor can use to assess and certify conformity.

Part 2: Guidance on the application of service management systems. This lists recommendations to support Part 1 and so is rather longer in length.

---

[1] Source: www.ISOIEC20000certification.com

Part 3: Guidance on scope definition and applicability of ISO/ IEC 20000-1. This is used to set the scope for an application for certification as not every part of an IT service department may need to demonstrate conformity.

Part 4: Service management process reference model. This sets out what processes are in scope and how they may be assessed for their maturity.

Part 5: Exemplar implementation plan. As the name implies, this is designed to help organisations implement an SMS to support certification to Part 1.

Part 10: Concepts and terminology. This is a glossary of the terms and definitions originally published in Part 1 but which has now been separated out in order to allow Part 1 to be focused on the conformity aspect.

Parts 6, 7, 8 and 9 remain work in progress aimed at providing an overall framework that will allow service management to be seen and used in conjunction with longer standing standards such as ISO 9001 and ISO 27001.

Whilst other standards can apply to service management, most notably ISO 9001 (Quality Management) and ISO 19770-1 (Software Asset Management), these are all becoming referenced through the ISO 20000 series framework and so need not be listed separately nor certification sought independently.

Whilst ISO/IEC 20000-1:2011 is the only **standard** that organisations can seek external recognition for achieving, there are other sources of good practice that a service desk can draw upon. For instance, COBIT 5, from ISACA[2] in the United States, is a framework that offers a detailed and comprehensive process reference guide to every aspect of IT. As COBIT 5 is broader than ISO 20000, it is often overlooked as a source of best practice guidance for SDIM, although it

---

[2] ISACA is the usual acronym of the Information Systems Audit and Control Association

includes incident management within the Deliver, Service and Support (DSS) domain as DSS4 – Manage Service Requests and Incidents. The scope of this is almost the same as that covered by the equivalent parts of ISO/IEC 20000-1:2011 and ITIL. COBIT is used mainly by auditors in highly regulated industries, such as banking, where there is a requirement to demonstrate IT governance, and so is not widely evidenced in other industry sectors or organisations operating mainly in Europe. As it is not a standard to which certification can be sought, there are no publicly available figures to indicate the extent to which this framework is used.

The third reference model outlined here, ITIL, is published as a framework of processes for service management that is based on what has been proven to work but is not designed to be prescriptive. ITIL does not apply only to particular industry sectors, as IT practices are commonplace across most types of organisation, and it does not rely on any specific technologies. The process descriptions can be adapted if necessary to suit the unique circumstances of the organisation that decides to use them, although – as these processes are based on known and proven practices – caution should be used if doing this. ITIL is also evolving and so is not a static framework.

It should be understood that COBIT and ITIL are not standards but reference guides for good practices. The ITIL process descriptions for incident management are often used by organisations seeking to achieve ISO 20000 compliance, but are not the only ones that can be used to gain certification. A brief comparison of the three reference frameworks is shown in Figure 4.1.

Figure 4.1 An overview of ITIL, COBIT and ISO 20000

> **ITIL** is a framework of best practices in IT service management documented in terms of the five phases of an overall ITSM lifecycle. ITIL processes can be customised if required to suit the needs of any IT service organisation.

(Continued)

Figure 4.1 (Continued)

> **COBIT** is an IT governance framework and associated tools that balance technical and process needs, business risks and control prerequisites. It integrates other standards and practices such as CMMI,[3] ISO 20000 and ITIL.
>
> **ISO 20000** is an international standard specifically covering IT service management and nothing else. It is the only standard against which an organisation can be independently audited and certification achieved.

All these frameworks will be of interest to a service desk operation and it is worth noting that ISO 20000 describes what needs to be demonstrated for incident management in just one page. It does not specify ITIL as the only source of best practice process definitions and, indeed, this need not be the case, although the changes made to ISO 20000 for the 2011 release have aligned its terminology with ITIL more than the 2005 edition did. For instance, ISO 20000, Clause 8.1, can be satisfied by applying the processes defined by the ITIL Incident Management and Service Request Management sections. So, what ISO 20000 now does is to incorporate the requirements of both incident and service request management as a single clause within the SMS to recognise that both types of work are normally carried out by the people working in a service desk capacity. This reflects actual practice.

An example of how COBIT or ITIL can help with the achievement of ISO 20000 would be to consider how an organisation should approach defining its service management ambitions before seeking certification. ISO 20000 is an SMS standard that specifies what needs to be put in place to fulfil all the requirements set out by a service provider. This is done by establishing the scope of the service to be assessed and, hence, what processes need to be evidenced – in the case of an SDIM

---

[3] CMMI stands for Capability Maturity Model Integration originated by Carnegie Mellon University in the US

operation, this would clearly include incident management. By referring to sources of good practice, such as COBIT and ITIL, the organisation seeking certification will be able to access independent and mature guidance on how processes should be designed, documented, managed and evidenced. As ISO 20000 requirements are generic, in that they apply to all service providers regardless of the type, size or nature of the service they manage, being able to refer to best practice frameworks having the same generic attributes makes sense. The scope of an ISO 20000 certificate covers the service provider by name, the type of service provided and what it consists of in terms of deliverables, but it does not include management of the function itself – so, in other words, the organisational structure is not part of the assessment process.

In order to summarise this section, it is important that we regard ITIL and COBIT as sources of good practice for guidance on how to approach SDIM and which may be used to help gain certification under ISO 20000 if required. Organisations cannot self-certify their own compliance to ISO 20000 and so an external, registered, independent certification body, of which there are several, should be approached for guidance on how registration can be achieved. These can be found by reference to the APM Group[4] who own and operate the organisational certification scheme and who list the registered certification bodies (known as RCBs) on their website. It is unusual to find an in-house service desk certified to ISO 20000 independently of the rest of the service management department unless the service desk operates autonomously – for instance, as a commercial organisation in its own right rather than as a function of a corporate IT department.

BEST PRACTICE FRAMEWORKS, PROCEDURES AND PROCESSES

As we have already described ITIL and COBIT as sources of good practice in the previous section, they will not be repeated here in the same way. What is important to bring out in this section

---

[4] The APM Group lists RCBs on the website http://isoiec20000certification.com/

is how service desk personnel should relate to processes to do their jobs and how these can be made both easy and consistent. The purpose of drawing on well-defined and published good practices is that they have already been proven to work in other organisations and so there would need to be a good reason to adapt them in anything other than a minor way. For example, an organisation might need to adapt processes if the needs of its application are so different from normal that good practice is not able to cope with it; however, this would be an extremely unusual situation. Every organisation supporting IT applications has broadly similar needs and this is why the management of them can be approached in standard ways. So we should proceed on the assumption that, regardless of the type of organisation concerned, good practices for SDIM will be drawn from documented and published sources such as ITIL or COBIT.

There are several ways that SDIM can access process descriptions, the obvious one being to buy the ITIL lifecycle publications that contain them – either the Service Operations manual alone or the whole suite if so desired. The whole 2011 suite of manuals may cost around £300 and the Service Operation one on its own sells for about £85. However, reading about ITIL processes as written words, either on paper or a screen, will only partly satisfy the need for them to be run reliably, consistently and effectively by a large group of staff over a long period of time. Unless these processes are implemented in a way which ensures that anyone using them is able to work in a defined manner over long periods, and able to achieve consistent results, the value of them can be seriously diminished, as described next.

Why processes need to be included in workflow

A project team took 18 months to carefully implement a new service desk system with incident management procedures published in paper form to all 30 staff working on the desk. However, each individual member of staff was able to manage incidents in whichever way

(Continued)

69

they felt was appropriate, depending on the department they were dealing with, as the service desk system did not enforce any particular workflow. As a result, the standards achieved by members of staff showed a high degree of individual variance and there was inconsistent attainment of the overall service targets that had been set. This placed an undue burden on the supervisors who were tasked with improving the service desk performance. A second project team needed to rework the implementation so that every member of staff worked to the same targets and used the same functions of the service desk system. However, the workflow still was not automated and so, once the second project team left site, performance fell away again leaving the supervisors with a similar problem, even though the provider of the service desk software tool was able to automate the procedures at little extra cost.

Documented process descriptions and operating procedures are absolutely essential to show how the processes operate and to define standard terms with an understanding of the purpose of the processes and their outcome. However, unless they provide ways in which they can be used in everyday work, their usefulness is limited and leads to the situation in the example above. So, something more than a text book or a PDF file is needed if the team are to work in a structured and consistent way, and this something is known as a process model or governance repository. Process models exist as pre-populated scripts that allow the best practice definitions from ITIL or other sources to be held in an electronic format so they can be presented as a reference to everyone who needs to access them. This means that any member of staff should be able to work through the screens presented to them without having to always decide what to do next, providing they have been suitably trained.

Whilst some workflow is provided in many ITSM tools, process models containing procedural guidance, and enforcement incorporated into the workflow, are still quite rare, which is unfortunate as incident management is a well-defined process that lends itself to rigorous and consistent presentation. As one of the key responsibilities of a service desk manager is to create a framework for the documentation of standards and KPIs, and to ensure adherence to them, as explained in Chapter 2, then it essential that they know how this can be achieved consistently. The process governance model described in this section represents what I believe to be one of the most advanced in the ITSM market and one of its features is that it can be deployed very quickly alongside the installation of an ITSM tool, or retrofitted to it if necessary.

Figure 4.2 is a representation of the GovernIT process model created by Partners in IT; it is designed to integrate seamlessly

Figure 4.2 An illustration of the overall process hierarchy in GovernIT, courtesy of John Perks.

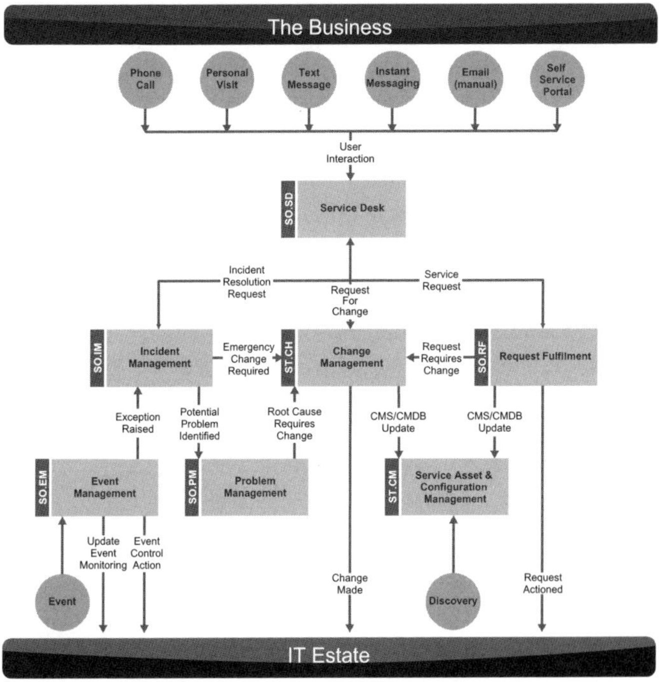

with a leading cloud-based toolset from an ITSM solution provider and can be adapted for others.

This cloud-based ITSM toolset is used by many organisations on the basis of its support for rapid deployment, intuitive workflow and cross-process integration, which is essential if service desk personnel are to work at high levels of efficiency. Being able to access process and procedural documentation at the same time is another feature that helps analysts do their job properly, as the implementation is designed to enforce and automate best practices without them needing to refer to offline resources.

GovernIT[5] is a governance repository that can be hosted either on site or as a cloud solution integrated with the tool, depending on customer needs. Either way, the documentation is accessed seamlessly from the tool and covers the main processes that are of interest to a service desk – incident management, request fulfilment and event management – as well as change management, problem management and configuration management that staff will also need in order to fit within the wider ITSM workflow. Figure 4.3 shows an example of how the GovernIT solution manages what is done; in this example the workflow is for the service request fulfilment process.

Once the GovernIT script is implemented with the ITSM tool, the screens available to service desk personnel are configured to present the workflow in a structured and consistent way and can provide guidance to staff at any point in the process. By means of another example, the extract in Table 4.1 consists of the documentation embedded within the process for incident management, and analysts can access lower-level detail at any time.

---

[5] More information on GovernIT is available from Partners in IT at www.piit.co.uk

Figure 4.3 An instance of the service request process flow within GovernIT
By courtesy of John Perks.

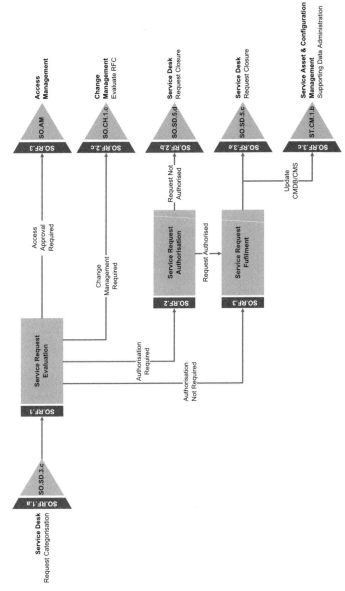

Table 4.1 An extract from the documentation for incident management in GovernIT

Role title	Text	Appears in pages
Incident Management (SOIM)		
Owner (Service Desk Analyst/ Operations Analyst)	• Checks new Requests or Events against Existing Incidents. • Relates new Requests or Events to existing Incidents where appropriate. • Maintains relationships between Requests, Events and Incidents. • Creates and populates Incident record. • Categorises and Prioritises Incident. • Maintains and updates Incident record. • Assigns Incident for investigation and resolution. • Escalates Major Incidents. • Invokes Major Incident communication plan. • Convenes Major Incident Board. • Closes Incidents.	Incident Management (SOIM) Incident Identification (SOIM01) Incident Categorisation & Prioritisation (SOIM02) Incident Closure (SOIM08)

(Continued)

Table 4.1 (Continued)

Role title	Text	Appears in pages
Incident Manager	• Manages Major Incidents. • Acts as the escalation point for all Incidents.	Incident Management (SOIM) Incident Categorisation & Prioritisation (SOIM02) Major Incident Initiation (SOIM03) Major Incident Investigation & Diagnosis (SOIM05) Major Incident Resolution & Recovery (SOIM07)
Service Owner	• Responsible for the accuracy of Service information.	Incident Management (SOIM) Incident Categorisation & Prioritisation (SOIM02)

(Continued)

Table 4.1 (Continued)

Role title	Text	Appears in pages
Team Coordinator	• Confirms relationships between Requests, Events and Incidents. • Ensures that the appropriate member of their team fulfils any assigned tasks. • Serves as an escalation point for the progression of tasks assigned to their team. • Communicates with the Incident Owner if tasks are wrongly assigned to their team, or if any of the associated information is incomplete. • Escalates Major Incidents. • Informs Incident Manager of Major Incident progress.	Incident Management (SOIM) Incident Identification (SOIM01) Incident Categorisation & Prioritisation (SOIM02) Major Incident Initiation (SOIM03) Investigation & Diagnosis (SOIM04) Major Incident Investigation & Diagnosis (SOIM05) Major Incident Resolution & Recovery (SOIM07)

(Continued)

Table 4.1 (Continued)

Role title	Text	Appears in pages
Technical Analyst	• Investigates and resolves Incidents. • Attempts to match Incidents to Problems. • Attempts to match Incidents to Changes. • Initiates Emergency Change when required. • Raises and completes Emergency Change records.	Incident Management (SOIM) Major Incident Initiation (SOIM03) Investigation & Diagnosis (SOIM04) Major Incident Investigation & Diagnosis (SOIM05) Resolution & Recovery (SOIM06) Major Incident Resolution & Recovery (SOIM07)

Using such automated process workflow with embedded documentation means that staff can reach high levels of productivity without needing constant offline referral to manuals. It also means that everyone will work to the same script and so individual performance variances will be minimised.

TOOLS

The previous section focused on process automation and scripting, although this is of no use without the availability of tools for them to work with. The service desk team will need to use various tools in order to do their jobs to the necessary standards of quality and efficiency, and examples of the type of tools that are widely used for SDIM include the following:

- An ITSM suite, products such as Service-Now, BMC Remedy or HP Service Manager, which will provide screens and the ability to log and record incidents and to monitor resolution against agreed SLA targets.

- An ACD system, supplied by companies such as Genesys, which will handle inbound telephone traffic and route it to the next available service desk analyst. The ACD may also be used to manage calls to a user to confirm they are willing for an incident too be closed once it is shown on the system as having been resolved.

- An asset discovery tool, for instance Atrium or Discovery, which can be run periodically or in the background to ensure that the configuration management database is kept up to date. The selection of this tool is not usually a service desk responsibility, but the service desk operation totally relies on the information that it provides. The resulting database update is offered to the incident management system so that an analyst can see what the service configuration looks like and what changes, if any, may have recently been made to it when trying to assess the likely cause of a reported fault.

- Remote takeover and management tools, such as Bomgar, which allows an analyst to take control of a user's PC to find out the exact nature of a reported issue.

- Performance monitoring tools, from companies like Nexthink, which show such things as network response time, application turnaround and website throughput to be displayed in real time so that, at a glance, analysts can see how the service infrastructure was working at the time of a reported incident.

• Event alerting and management tools, from BMC or Compuware, which show the possibility of something about to happen that may not be immediately service-affecting but could be classed as an incident in the near future and so needs addressing in some way.

• Reporting tools, such as Performance Analytics, which present information in terms of SLAs, OLAs, KPIs and other metrics to both the service desk and the wider IT organisation as a measure of how well the operation is being managed.

There are many tools available that can fulfil the needs described above, but as the remit of this book is people and how they interact with processes rather than any technology solutions, it would be inappropriate to do other than mention some examples – technology changes quickly, whereas people and process do so more slowly. The tools used to manage specific aspects of a service, such as remote takeover, are usually known as domain managers as they are often device-dependent, working with named products and often from the same manufacturers, although independent products are available.

The framework shown in Figure 4.4 is an example of an integrated ITSM suite deployed in an organisation with multiple technology towers – different vendors or product suites – but with a common service desk operation using shared incident and service request management instances.

It can be seen that the heart of the operation is a shared service desk that operates a number of processes, in this instance including problem management and change management although the service desk manager was not the process owner for these last two. The workflow between processes was managed partly by the ITSM suite itself and partly by the type of process model described in the last section – Best

Figure 4.4 A model of an ITSM framework integrating multiple toolsets and processes

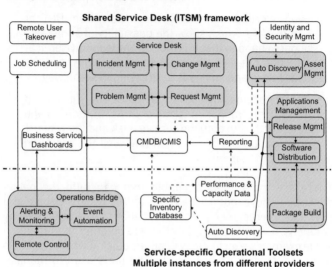

**Service-specific Operational Toolsets
Multiple instances from different providers**

Practice Frameworks, Procedures and Processes – and each service provider, of which there were four in this example, managed their own activities within the framework using common standards known as APIs (Application Programming Interfaces). This ensured that the service desk team, the incident management and service request management processes could all initiate service referrals to any of the four outsourced providers and respond to operational alerts.

The choice of ITSM suite and associated domain management tools is a complex one as it depends on the type of hardware and software being used by the organisation. This choice is often made by a project team working with the service desk team as a client, or, in some cases, the service desk manager will be the project owner and so takes responsibility for product evaluation and selection. Whichever method is used, the SDIM team need to agree the way forward as they are the ones who will have to use it for many years to come. Some tools will work with different technologies, whereas others are specific to just one type of product or vendor. The same situation applies to ITSM suites themselves, not all of which can support every ITIL process.

An example of a third-party organisation that provides impartial and independent ITIL assessments of ITSM toolsets is Pink Elephant through their PinkVERIFY[6] service, which assesses the degree to which a toolset supports the processes defined by ITIL 2011 as well as the various earlier versions. This is publicly available and, at the time of writing, there are 28 vendors or products listed by PinkVERIFY that have been submitted for assessment. However, not every vendor submits themselves or their products to the PinkVERIFY assessment process so, like any awards scheme, the choice is self-selecting and the products themselves offer varying degrees of ITIL process support – from the most functional offering of 15 verified ITIL processes, to the most focused, with just one process. However, one product of these 28 is not verified for incident management at all and so there are clearly choices to be made from the remaining 27 based on such factors as cost, complexity and ease of use as well as their ability to link through well-defined APIs into the various domain management tools that will also be needed.

The implementation of an ITSM tool to support the creation or enhancement of a service desk operation is usually handled by means of a formally defined project. This is because there is investment to be made, service benefits to be realised and a new method of working to be established to match the design brief. Every ITSM project is different and, whilst it is unusual to find the service desk manager running such a project, this does happen in smaller organisations, although there will be a separate project team in larger companies. The brief for any project initiation will need to take account of the vision for the service desk operation as well as service availability by day of week and hour of day to be offered and the service levels that need to be achieved.

---

[6] The results of assessments using PinkVERIFY are available through
www.pinkelephant.com

Many ITSM toolsets are now available in both purchasable product and subscription service formats, so the capital outlay can be managed more flexibly than in the past. However, any such project will usually need to show a return on investment, even if the expenditure consists mainly of revenue rather than capital outlay, as the overall cost can still be significant. It is worth running any ITSM tool implementation as a project in order to bring in the disciplines associated with business case management and benefits realisation as means of quantifying the value of a service desk. A properly managed service desk implementation will show a positive return on investment based on both IT and on user service value.

5 CAREER PROGRESSION AND RELATED ROLES

CAREER PROGRESSION

There is not one unique career path defined for a service desk manager and people filling this type of role can come to it from a variety of other jobs. As we explored in chapters 2 and 3, the main attributes for success – and survival – in this demanding role are the ability to work under pressure, a strong sense of customer empathy, plus persistence when dealing with other people in IT who have responsibility for resolving incidents that have been assigned to them. In larger teams, good people-management skills are also vitally important as the incident-management resources working on the front line will exhibit workload pressures, training issues, rude customers and having to deal with matters that may be outside their normal experiences. As a result, staff turnover can be high – up to 25 per cent per annum – but after all, this is a front line service job which is not for the faint hearted. However, it is often used as a career step to other IT roles and the experiences of two service desk managers are described in Chapter 6 which explain where they came from, how they managed their workload and how doing that job helped their subsequent IT careers.

Jobs in SDIM are often, but not always, seen as an entry level to the IT department. Many people come to work in this area from jobs in operational departments or from roles that need good customer skills and the ability to keep calm under pressure, and it is important that everyone works to the same profile regardless of their background. It is helpful to use a template to match the skills that individuals have against an industry standard and so we will use SFIA*plus* as the basis for a discussion on how to progress within an SDIM hierarchy. SFIA*plus* contains the international SFIA skills and competency framework that describes IT roles, and adds detailed training and development resources to it such that both employers and staff can use it for career planning and training purposes. It has been adopted by companies and government bodies across the world, and SFIA is supported in the UK by all the professional bodies with an interest in ITSM. We can see from Table 5.1 how this works. Each seniority step in the SFIA matrix subsumes the level beneath it; so, for example, someone working at SFIA Level 5 – the manager – will be expected to have gained proficiency at the various tasks for a Level 4 (supervisory) post before being able to take on wider responsibilities. This is obviously wise as every job needs to understand the constraints and opportunities afforded by their subordinates.

Table 5.1 The skills hierarchy for service desk career progression

Category	Service Management Skills	Code	Level						
			1	2	3	4	5	6	7
Service operation	Service desk & incident management	USUP	1	2	3	4	5		

Reproduced by kind permission of the SFIA Foundation.

The advantage of using SFIA*plus* as a career template is that the characteristics of each level are the same regardless of which job is being looked at – so, a Level 3 job in one discipline is the equal of a Level 3 job in another. The technical aspects of two jobs at the same level may be different – for instance, between two different disciplines – but the background, personal and accountability dimensions are the same across all the SFIA defined skills. Using the SFIA levels means that people can plan their careers as a number of vertical, horizontal or diagonal steps without having to wait for a more senior role in the team they are currently assigned to. Whilst not everyone will aspire to a Level 7 post, there is no restriction in planning terms as to what can be achieved by using a formal skills matrix.

Some people progress their careers entirely through working in progressively more senior service desk roles, as one of the case studies did as explained in Chapter 6. This affords the individual a known route to fulfil their managerial ambitions, although taking supervisory responsibility for people who were previously your peers will mean that you need the attributes to be able to deal with this sensitively. There is significant benefit in moving from a tier 1 analyst (SFIA Level 2) to a tier 2 analyst (SFIA Level 3) as this involves dealing with more demanding incidents and offers a good introduction to the art of developing procedures. However, many staff working on a service desk will be in transit from one type of IT job towards another, with the experiences of working on the front line seen as an important milestone in their careers rather than an end in itself. The other case study in Chapter 6 shows an example of someone who came to the service desk manager role as a sideways transfer from infrastructure support, which, as a technical specialist, meant that he was able to impart good problem solving and PC skills to his teams. Other managers working on a service desk come to the job as a way of developing managerial skills, perhaps from a project background, before seeing how to develop a wider role in a related discipline. Whatever background an individual has before entering the service desk, they will end up learning more about human nature and the way that an organisation works than by doing just about any other job in IT.

It is not necessary even to have experience in IT before joining a service desk, as attitudes and customer orientation matter more than pure technical capability, which can either be learned or acquired through clever scripting within the ITSM tool's process set or Knowledge Base. The SFIA description for the manager's job at Level 5 suggests that the incumbent can have gained experience, typically for four or more years, as a competent user of computer systems, some of which should have been in a position of responsibility. They need to show a good understanding of how such systems work within the business and have a lot of experience of handling user contact, which means that staff from a high-street branch of a retailer or bank will fit the bill. I have had positive experiences of appointing branch personnel to service desk roles as the customer feedback on how the interaction was handled was often higher than when dealing with an IT technician doing the same job. The individuals concerned will be looking for an entry to the IT department and a service desk job is a good one for them to consider.

Once you start to progress a career in IT, you will quickly discover that without support it will be difficult to find out exactly what is needed from you. Annual appraisals may provide the input needed in terms of training and development needs, although that happens less often than is necessary. Annual appraisals are also, understandably, heavily focused on the job as it exists today rather than how the employee should view their skills in terms of a future job. I have always worked on the 'principle of thirds' for any employee to use as a guide to career planning, on the basis that no-one ends up doing the same job when they retire as when they started work. This principle works by giving weight to how someone does a job in three ways:

- what your past job provided in terms of your skills and experience;
- what the current job needs from you in order to demonstrate success;
- what your next role will need in order to help plan your development.

The weighting of these three factors will depend where you are in the job cycle – after first being appointed to a job, the emphasis will naturally be more on stage 1 than stage 3. Following a satisfactory trial period, the emphasis will move to stage 2 whereas when being actively considered for promotion stage 3 will take a more prominent role. There is no arithmetic rule that governs these weightings as each organisation will have policies for appraisals and organisational development and each team will have its own way of dealing with recruits who join it.

An example from a different industry, the police service, might help to illustrate this principle. Some senior ranks of police officer are eligible for fast track promotion by taking the academic qualifications of a candidate into account alongside their experience in either the police or a related industry and where this combination might be of most value to the service. This means that a fast track candidate need not necessarily have spent years on the beat to qualify for a management position providing this is handled in a structured way, and is obviously only viable if a formal succession template exists.

So, it is important to have some form of 'big picture' that shows how each job needs to have a progressively deeper and richer set of skills as it develops. One way of showing this in IT is illustrated in Figure 5.1, which describes development relevant to the seven IT job levels by means of activities which broaden ability beyond the minimum needed to fulfil the current role.

Figure 5.1 Professional development activities relevant to the seven IT job levels, courtesy of Roy Shepherd

Levels		1	2	3	4	5	6	7
Increasing Knowledge								
PDFK01	Additional Study	X	X					
PDFK02	Gaining Knowledge of Employing Organisation	X	X	X				
PDFK03	Gaining Knowledge of Surrounding Technical Areas	X	X	X				
PDFK04	'Research' Assignments			X	X	X		

(Continued)

Figure 5.1 (Continued)

Levels		1	2	3	4	5	6	7
PDFK05	Gaining Knowledge of Activities of Employing Organisation				X	X		
PDFK06	Gaining Knowledge of ICT Concepts and Techniques				X	X		
PDFK07	Gaining Knowledge of Broader ICT Issues					X	X	X
PDFK08	Gaining Strategic Knowledge of Employing Organisation					X	X	X
PDFK09	Gaining Knowledge of Standards and Legislation						X	X
Developing Professional Skills								
PDFS01	Time Management		X	X				
PDFS02	Team Working		X	X				
PDFS03	Communications		X	X				
PDFS04	Negotiating and Influencing				X	X		
PDFS05	Team Leadership				X	X		
PDFS06	Management Development					X	X	
PDFS07	General Management						X	X
Broadening Activities								
PDFB01	Participation in Group Activities	X	X	X				
PDFB02	Extra Mural Activities	X	X	X	X	X	X	
PDFB03	Extra Mural Studies			X	X	X	X	
PDFB04	Deputising				X	X		

(Continued)

Figure 5.1 (Continued)

Levels		1	2	3	4	5	6	7
PDFB05	Job Rotation and Special Assignments				X	X	X	
PDFB06	Community Work				X	X	X	X
PDFB07	Project Assignments					X	X	
PDFB08	Mentoring					X	X	
PDFB09	International Experience					X	X	X
Participation in Professional Activities								
PDFP01	Attendance at Professional Body Activities	X	X	X				
PDFP02	Participation in Professional Body Affairs				X	X	X	X
PDFP03	Publications				X	X	X	X
PDFP04	Teaching and Tutoring				X	X	X	X
PDFP05	Standards and Legislation					X	X	X
Total		6	9	10	13	20	16	10

Figure 5.1 is divided into four groupings as follows:

- increasing knowledge;
- developing professional skills;
- broadening activities;
- participation in professional activities.

There is considerable overlap between these categories and therefore allocation of an activity to a category is not prescriptive. The levels shown are those at which it would be most appropriate to undertake the activity listed.

The reference numbers in the first column refer to specific development needs; so, for example, PDFK01 – Additional Study – means building on initial education through additional study by means of distance learning, evening classes or day release courses, and it can be seen that this is specifically aimed at levels 1 and 2. Activities appropriate for Level 5, the service desk manager, could include PDFS06 – Management Development – which involves the individual undertaking training and practice in, and gaining, an understanding of the skills and techniques required to manage all or part of an organisation, including business and financial management, management of change and strategic planning. This will require both on- and off-the-job training and may include participation in an appropriate development programme such as an MBA. As a means of explaining what is needed to succeed in a job at any particular level, this matrix is particularly helpful.

Not only does use of this type of matrix add diversity but it also helps to explain why the skills of SDIM are spread across five different levels and rewarded accordingly. Some of these skills may be given to staff as development objectives, and, on a very large service desk, some staff will act in a role supporting projects going live in order to define the support procedures. This will count as a contribution towards their eventual job progression.

Some of these development activities can be gained through IT-specific courses and events, whereas others are of a more general nature. The levels in SFIA*plus* broadly correspond to other professional qualifications based on a seven-level framework, such as the National Occupational Standards for Management and Leadership – or NOS for short. These standards are now managed by SkillsCFA[1] alongside the National Vocational Qualifications (NVQs) and the Scottish Vocational Qualifications (SVQs) which include skills specific to contact centres.

---

[1] The SkillsCFA website is http://skillscfa.org/

The NOS standards were developed to provide a 'best practice' benchmark, and SkillsCFA ensure they are kept fit for the purpose for which they were developed. The current NOS standards include reference to the behaviours that underpin effective performance at different levels of capability, including the levels that service desk personnel are interested in, most notably levels 3, 4 and 5. This is because organisations increasingly understand that the soft skills which people need in their jobs are as important at getting the job done as the specific technical attributes – regardless of the discipline in question. Using these standards as a benchmark is a way of helping to address the prerequisites described in Figure 5.1 that anyone looking at SFIAplus will need to address in order to satisfy the needs of the role they are interested in.

Individuals can use these standards to understand the skills that are needed for a particular role, to help them assess what they may already have and to plan for the acquisition of new skills. The CPD portal that will be described in the Continuing Professional Development section of this chapter will help with the process but not the actual qualifications themselves. In this respect, it is useful that people planning a career move look at the CMI qualifications which are aligned to the NOS, such as a Level 3 qualification in first line management or a Level 5 qualification in leadership and management. These qualifications match the equivalent levels in SFIAplus and can be viewed in more detail through the CMI website,[2] from which fact sheets relating to the different qualifications and levels can be downloaded free of charge. As well as providing detail on the contents and credits available for each type of award, these fact sheets also provide a cross match of each qualification to the units in NOS, for example NOS Unit D3 (Recruit, Select and Keep Colleagues) appears as a component in Unit 3006 (Recruitment and Selection) and Unit 3008 (Improving Team Performance) of the CMI Level 3 Diploma in First Line Management. Gaining such qualifications can satisfy SFIAplus requirements for the appropriate level.

---

[2] The CMI website is www.managers.org.uk

RELATED ROLES

The service desk will interact not only with customers but also with other jobs in IT, as we saw in Chapter 3. So it is not uncommon for staff to move between the functions that work together on a daily basis, for instance to and from change management or a tier 2 resolver group such as desktop support. Many of the incidents logged are related to desktop PCs, laptops or smart phones and their applications, so it is understandable that staff see a move from one function to another as being a natural developmental step.

Other IT roles that the service desk will interact with are service managers or business relationship managers, but these are not defined under the service desk structure. Both of these type of jobs exist to manage the relationship that a service provider has with their customer – the service manager role being to deal with service provision on a day-to-day basis by attending meetings, linking customer needs to the service plan and by dealing with issues on escalation. They are not usually subordinate to the service desk, and typically carry management responsibility, but they relate very strongly to the work that the desk does as they draw on incident data to inform them about which customers have been affected and why. Often, organisations that have service managers deploy them as major incident managers to relieve the incident management team of this responsibility once such an event occurs.

Business relationship management occupies the Client Interface part of the SFIA matrix. These jobs are divided into sales and marketing and client support disciplines, with the latter one being an area of particular relevance. Account management, or relationship management, exists to manage the overall commercial activity that an IT department has with its customers – not just the service aspects. This may mean dealing not only with escalations of concern but also the claw back of payments as a result of non-attainment of SLAs, which are usually dealt with by means of service credits – so many points accumulated as a service credit can be translated into a sum to be repaid at the end of a financial accounting period. For this reason, the linkage between a service desk manager and account managers is a fundamental one to get right as continual application of service credits could lead to the budget for the service desk being reduced – a downward spiral if overwork is the underlying cause.

It could also involve the customer organisation, regardless of whether it is part of the same business entity or not, serving notice that an alternative service desk provider needs to be found. This is not uncommon and so the relationship that a service desk manager has with their account management counterparts, who will be of a similar or greater managerial level, is clearly important. The service desk manager should not be so bogged down with dealing with technical calls that their team cannot manage, or dealing with escalation issues, to such an extent that they do not allocate time to meet and discuss the service landscape with their business facing colleagues. After all, this is a potential career move – either way round – but it is more often the case that a service desk manager will move into a business relationship role as it usually offers a greater freedom to act.

One related role that is also very important for the service desk team to understand and promote is that of a **power user**. This is not one that can be formally defined, but anyone working in the IT industry will recognise that many user departments will have someone who their colleagues prefer to deal with in respect of IT issues than the IT service desk. Do not worry about this – encourage them whilst managing the way in which incidents are handled in conjunction with these individuals. They are sometimes also known as **super users** and, whilst they could be regarded as dangerous individuals if provided with any form of system administration rights, there is a positive benefit in supporting and promoting their existence.

Let us take a real example where power users worked to the benefit of IT. A leading international company devolved responsibility for some aspects of executive directors, IT support to their personal assistants (PAs), a potentially controversial move as it involved granting them a degree of control that would usually have resided only on the service desk. The aspects of control that were ceded to this group were service request management – so they could directly order phones or laptop accessories for their bosses without going through IT – and access management so they could arrange for their bosses to use systems in one country even when they were only set up for another. This worked to IT's benefit since it was clear that neither the directors nor their PAs could work effectively within the constraints of a commodity provision SLA and, importantly, the demands that very senior staff can make on an IT help desk may distort the support given to operational users. What it also provided, as a collateral benefit, was that IT was thought of much more favourably by ceding this degree of control to them rather than trying to hang on to a centralised service provision model. Of course, there were issues and concerns that needed to be addressed in order to make sure that the PAs worked within a controlled framework rather than being been given complete freedom to do whatever they liked, but the balance that was struck worked for all parties – and IT was better thought of as a result.

Such arrangements work well for this type of VIP user as the context for a service issue or advice request cannot always be easily described to a tier 1 analyst. This may be because the situation cannot be characterised by a simple commodity product request, but more often than not the executive concerned may simply not be trying to use their equipment as it was designed to be used – and it can be best for their PA to coach them rather than someone from IT. It is therefore wise for the service desk to establish a degree of devolution over some matters concerning VIP support even if the desk can offer it. Supporting such a service, especially in the case of the BYOD (bring your own device) world where individuals often prefer to talk to a colleague in preference to IT, is better than allowing a shadow IT department to be formed. Supporting VIP devolution, where appropriate, with process, procedure and a good knowledge base, rather than trying to prevent it, will improve relationships as well as increase the likelihood of the service desk being regarded as adding organisational value.

CONTINUING PROFESSIONAL DEVELOPMENT

Career progression in any type of job needs to be based on some form of record that demonstrates what someone has done to get to where they claim to be. This record can be as informal as relevant experience being written down on a CV or even just described verbally, but that no longer supports the professionalism agenda which increasingly seeks evidence to show not just what has been achieved but how that experience was gained.

SFIA*plus* allows very structured career development, as we have seen in the previous section, by means of its seven-level model and embedded training and skill requirements for each level and every job type working at that level. But SFIA*plus* by itself does not provide a formal way to document CPD and so some means of being able to plan for, and record, the achievement of your goals, skills and experiences is required. This can be by means of a training plan which either the IT or HR department can manage, although this on its own may not provide enough detail on why a particular training intervention was requested or what will happen as a consequence of you having received it. This is where use of a mechanism such as a CPD recording tool can help, in conjunction with the career and professional development support and training outcomes outlined in the previous section. A CPD tool is a means of helping individuals to achieve their career aspirations by allowing the use of frameworks such as SFIA*plus* and specific training topics to plan, and then demonstrate, achievement of a career plan. A documented CPD record will enable individuals to improve their chances of getting another job by being able to demonstrate how the skills to succeed at that role have been gained and how willing you are to do more – all in the context of an agreed plan.

There are different types of CPD activity, which can be summarised as:

- how you are dealing with your current job – especially the challenges;
- working with 'stretch goals' – often used to develop to a bigger job;
- evidence of dealing with a new job or planning to take on an new job;
- academic qualifications, gained either on the job or by formal study;
- professional qualifications, such as practitioner or chartership levels;
- attendance at events and conferences, perhaps even as a speaker.

An illustration of a typical CPD cycle is shown in Figure 5.2.

Figure 5.2 A typical CPD cycle

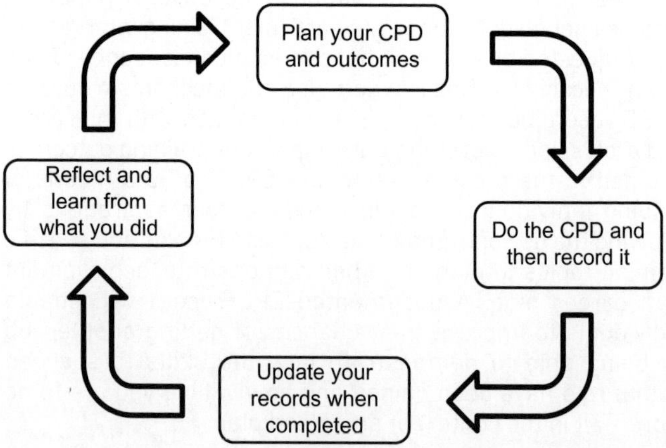

Use of a CPD recording tool is a useful way of demonstrating competence and commitment when you get called for an interview. If the interview is at a company which has not got another way of evaluating professionalism, it can help you to describe what you have achieved and why. People conducting interviews also need to understand what questions they need to ask and what the answers may mean, which is why the information in the next section will be of interest to both applicants and interviewers for service desk roles.

One aspect of training that has been mentioned in earlier sections is that concerned with gaining specific ITSM qualifications. Whilst it is not essential that people coming to a job on a service desk already have specific ITSM qualifications, it is very important that they be gained at the appropriate time in order to fully satisfy the role. Accredited examination institutes, such as BCS, EXIN and APMG, offer a wide range of qualifications in ITSM topics that are structured across four ascending levels, as follows:

- Foundation level;
- Intermediate or Specialist level;
- ITIL Expert;
- ITIL Master.

The levels most appropriate for a service desk are Foundation and Specialist, as the scope and depth of both the Expert and Master qualifications are too great. The Foundation Certificate in IT Service Management is the most common and valuable qualification that anyone looking to succeed in a service desk or incident management job should possess, and, as its name implies, it lays down the basics of terminology and emphasis regardless of likely future ITSM roles. Other qualifications appropriate to tiers 1 and 2 service desk analysts could include Microsoft Certified Solutions Expert (MCSE) or other specific technology vendors', or even regulatory body, accreditations, depending on which industry sector the organisation works within.

However, these general certifications act as a platform for a more specific qualification for service desk personnel; namely, the Specialist Certificate in Service Desk and Incident Management[3] – or SDIM for short. This sits above Foundation level, like the mainstream ITIL Intermediate level qualifications, but, unlike its intermediate counterparts, is job specific. It has been designed to reflect general industry best practices used within ITSM – and specifically SDIM – and aligns to ISO 20000, ITIL, COBIT and SFIA, the service management standard and frameworks that have already been described.

It can be seen that, for all the jobs described in this book, this particular qualification, along with the Foundation Certificate in Service Management, which is a prerequisite for it anyway, will satisfy many of the professional development needs of anyone looking to succeed as a service desk manager.

DEALING WITH INTERVIEWS AND ASSESSMENTS

Possessing technical and professional certifications is very important, but being able to produce certificates and diplomas will not of itself get you a job. This comes down to how you will be appraised when applying for a job, which will usually be based on a mixture of interview and assessment techniques. Whilst a general discussion of the use of assessment centres would be inappropriate in the case of a service desk manager, it is felt that some background on interviews and the assessment of personal characteristics is important. The questions used at a job interview will typically be based on a mixture of organisation-specific issues, such as what a candidate knows about the business, and skills-based questions to find out how the new job would be approached. Organisations with good HR policies may already have a standard template for the former, but, as the scope of this book is about the service desk, we will concentrate on the skills-based aspects of an interview – both job specific and also about the personal attributes needed. This latter area is especially important for management jobs.

---

[3] http://certifications.bcs.org/content/ConTab/54

Table 5.2 shows a typical interview question and the sources of evidence for the skills that a good candidate for a service desk supervisor's position would be expected to display. The presentation shown in this table would not be given to the interviewers on the day, but are evidence pointers in order for the candidate to explain the approach that he or she would take in that scenario.

Table 5.2 A typical interview question and sources of evidence for interviewers

Interview question	Skills indicators / evidence
You are managing a team of second-line analysts, who will shortly be brought on to a new Service Desk tool. They will then be expected to follow ITIL Incident Management policy and process. Their experience of ITIL is variable (though generally relatively low). They may also be hostile to changes in their working practices. You have 10 minutes to describe to them the ITIL incident lifecycle, and the advantages of logging and managing incidents using a single logging system and standard process. You should also address concerns that you anticipate that they may have about this change.	Knowledge of ITIL processes and how they impact on the role of the service desk, and specifically Incident Management. Has excellent oral and written communication skills and is able to work at all levels of the organisation. Can acquire information and identify gaps in the available information required to understand a problem or situation and devise a means of remedying such gaps. Proposed presentation should be expected to include the following:

(Continued)

Table 5.2 (Continued)

Interview question	Skills indicators / evidence

Please explain how you would go about doing this and the benefits.	• Why the change is necessary, what they will change to and how the change will be effected, when and by whom;
	
	• What will it mean for the individual analyst;
	
	• Adverse indicators for service needing to be remedied.
	
	• Benefits of ITIL to organisation are:
	  ▪ reduced costs;
	  ▪ improved IT services through the use of proven best practice processes;
	  ▪ improved customer satisfaction through a more professional approach to service delivery;
	  ▪ standards and guidance;
	  ▪ improved productivity;
	  ▪ improved use of skills and experience; and
	  ▪ improved delivery of third-party services through the specification of ITIL or ISO 20000 as the standard for service delivery in services procurements.

(Continued)

Table 5.2 (Continued)

Interview question	Skills indicators / evidence

	• Benefits to the individual could be:
	  ▪ focus should be on what people have to gain by the new approach rather than what they are losing;
	  ▪ emphasis on quality, consistency, continuous improvement, clarity;
	  ▪ individual contribution moving up the value chain, which enriches the roles;
	  ▪ a higher level of skill is required and so it is career enhancing work.

This question covers all the procedural and specific ITIL topics and it would be normal to expect someone coming for interview, especially if they have been part of a major shortlisting exercise, to score highly on both aspects. But that can just represent 'head knowledge', or what you know rather than what you can do, and so, as a service desk job is on the front line, more specific personal qualities will also be required. This is where many well intentioned recruitment exercises fall short, as they concentrate on the achievement of certifications and convincing PowerPoint presentations rather than selecting a candidate being able to do the job 24/7. They can also focus too much on filling a vacancy quickly – a common issue in ITSM.

Assuming that candidates have been able to satisfy the job requirements in terms of qualifications and approach to the job as outlined in Table 5.2, it then needs to be seen whether their personal characteristics are also appropriate. The role of the service desk manager is crucial to ITSM as it is the customer 'face' of IT and manages the people that handle incidents.

The role therefore needs to have a range of qualities, skills and experience to be successful – not just knowledge about IT applications, technology and infrastructure, but also business skills, people management, customer service and third-party supplier management. Knowledge of IT systems, processes and procedures can be more easily learned through study, whereas the skills required to lead and manage people, customers and suppliers are largely dependent upon experience, training and development and are often innate personal characteristics. So an assessment for someone applying to be a manager or supervisor will need to take account of 'soft', or less detailed, skills as well as the obvious IT ones. Examples of such skills that interviewers are likely to need to be aware of are:

- What knowledge does the candidate have of the business within which the service desk is providing a service?

- How well developed are the candidate's interpersonal and communication skills?

- Does the candidate display personal characteristics such as resolve, flexibility, emotional resilience and a good sense of humour?

A more specific set of skills, and the evidence that should be sought to assess how candidates present them, is provided for reference in the Appendix.

In considering the size of each role to determine its value and peer-group relationship in an organisation, it is worth remembering that job evaluation is not a science but a technique based on judgement. With this in mind, it is important to look at the key dimensions of a role that deliver successful performance. This will take account of the breadth and depth of the knowledge required, the interaction of the role with other IT jobs, the level and type of the interaction, the structure and controls within which the role operates and the overall impact of the role on the organisation. In the case of a service desk manager, the job requires both IT and business knowledge at a conceptual level rather than just an extensive practical 'doing' level, although there is significant managerial content across a range of disciplines which will require practical operational expertise. This plays to the requirement for people skills and the interaction of the role with others – these are critical for the role and the achievement of its objectives. The environment within which SDIM operates is usually well established with policies and procedures, but there does remain some discretion for action due to the unknown potential of, in particular, major incident or VIP incident management. In view of this, the job has significant potential to either beneficially or adversely impact the business depending upon the correct identification of an issue, the response of the team, the deployment of resources, the elapsed time and the satisfactory restoration of a service.

Some of these personal qualities can be assessed at interview, whereas others – such as resilience, stamina, sense of humour and keeping calm under pressure – are traits that a good candidate will probably display in their current job. So it is strongly recommended that, wherever possible, these are checked with the previous department or employer. This is straightforward in terms of an internal appointment, whereas it is much more difficult to get such information from another employer. For the manager's job in particular, it is common practice to use some kind of behavioural type test when a candidate is coming from another organisation in order to establish what their preferred working environment and style is likely to be. HR or the training functions of larger IT organisations will use such techniques for in-house staff and these can also be used for external recruits. Candidates need to be aware if such assessment techniques are to be used as part of the selection process as they are extra to an interview.

Pay rates for SDIM jobs vary widely across the country and by type of employing organisation. Examples of pay rates encountered during assignments are shown in Table 5.3. However, these are not standardised, as small companies can pay below the minimum and companies in, say, Central London may need to pay above the maximum. As is the case for any salary expectations, the experiences of different people in different companies are influenced by organisational culture and job design – sometimes the service desk and incident team do other work as well as perform their core role. This can influence how they are rewarded.

Table 5.3 Typical salaries paid to permanent service desk staff

JOB TYPE	LOCATION	SALARY RANGE	
		Minimum	Maximum
Service Desk Manager	London and South East	£35,000	£50,000
	Midlands and North	£26,000	£45,000
	Scotland and NI	£25,000	£40,000
Tier 2 Service Desk analyst	London and South East	£25,000	£45,000
	Midlands and North	£22,000	£40,000
	Scotland and NI	£19,000	£30,000
Tier 1 Service Desk analyst	London and South East	£18,000	£30,000
	Midlands and North	£15,000	£24,000
	Scotland and NI	£15,000	£25,000

In the case of the manager's position, the salaries achieved by individuals confirm that the job is viewed as a peer with other senior IT jobs and that, as a potential Chartered IT Professional (CITP), it should command commensurate pay.

The salaries paid to contract or outsourced staff may differ from the ones shown in Table 5.3, but in all cases salaries need to be aligned to both the structure of the employing organisation and at an appropriate rate for the type of business they work in. You are strongly advised to use current salary data from organisations that specialise in this field.[4] However, they offer average and general advice that may not suit your organisation.

---

[4] Salary data can be obtained, sometimes at a cost, from the following specialists:
http://reed.co.uk/average-salary/it-telecoms
http://cwjobs.co.uk/salary-checker/salary-calculator
http://hays.co.uk/it-salary-guide/HAYS_717802
http://uk.hudson.com/salary-surveys

6 SERVICE DESK MANAGER CASE STUDIES

Everything that has been described so far is based on what a job on a service desk involves, how it should be approached and the qualifications and qualities that are needed in order to perform well in that environment. This has introduced a diverse range of topics ranging from tools and processes through to skills, interview questions and personal qualities, which have never before been drawn together in this form. But what should be of interest to you would be to learn about how some real-life service desk managers found the role they worked in and how they responded to the various challenges and opportunities they faced. I asked two people to provide their perspectives on the job of a service desk manager and their answers are shown in the following sections. They are different in two respects – one came to the job 'through the ranks' of tier 1 and then tier 2 support, whereas the other came to the job from a technical management role. They also worked in different industry sectors, which many will think means a different job, but, as you will see, their challenges and experiences were broadly the same.

Whilst these differences are interesting, what will be even more relevant to anyone currently working as a service desk manager, or aspiring to be one, is that some years of working in these jobs fitted them for more senior jobs in IT as the management and business exposure the service desk provided proved to be good for their career development. They are both successful IT professionals. The interviews are quoted more or less verbatim as it was felt an important benefit to you was that the stories could be 'heard' in their own words.

THE WORK OF THE SERVICE DESK MANAGER OF A MAJOR RETAIL CHAIN

Q **What was your job title?**
A Service Desk Manager – Retail.

Q **What got you up in the morning and sent you home at night knowing that you had done a good job?**
A Knowing that every day was going to have a different set of challenges. No two days in succession were ever the same and, to me, a good job meant that knowing no fires were left burning from either an incident or people perspective when I came to go home.

Q **What background did you have before joining a service desk?**
A I trained initially as an electrical engineer and then studied programming before working for a small IT company. I wanted career advancement so applied to work as a tier 1 analyst. I liked the work and was good at resolving incidents and so advanced to tier 2 after a few years and then became a team leader. I was eventually promoted to manage the Retail service desk looking after every store in the country.

Q **What knowledge, skills and experience have been of most value in helping you to succeed?**
A Understanding what makes the people in your team tick and understanding their strengths is important, as is listening to them when things go wrong as they will probably know why it did.

Building relationships with other people at all levels in the organisation, both inside and outside of IT.

Addressing performance issues promptly – your team will be stronger for it.

Encouraging the sharing, rather than the hoarding of knowledge.

Ensuring that everyone has the opportunity for development, even if it means letting them work in another team for a couple of weeks so they can learn new skills.

Q **What was your workload like?**

A We supported over 14,000 tills and 8,000 PCs used by over 50,000 staff in 2,500 stores. This estate generated 1,300 calls a day, about 60% of these needing to be converted to incidents.

Q **So not a Monday–Friday job then?**

A Absolutely not – the hours of service were 12 hours a day on weekdays, 10 hours on Saturday and 9 hours every Sunday. Outside that time Operations could take calls on our behalf. I had 28 people to manage this workload within published KPIs.

Q **How did you relate to other managers in IT and what type of meetings did you attend?**

A I attended the CAB [Change Advisory Board] which was essential. I had a fantastic relationship with the Change Manager which was based on trust. Sometimes he was put in a position by a high-profile project that was poorly planned but that couldn't be rejected otherwise IT would be seen in a negative light so I would manage the impact on and communication with the service desk team to prepare for the inevitable issues. Also, if I said no to an initiative because we couldn't sensibly support it then he would take that from me at face value and reject the change as being too high risk.

I also went to any meetings that gave me visibility of projects or other releases being planned – as forewarned is to be forearmed!

Regular meetings with the service managers were essential as they were closer to the customer than to IT and so we needed to stay closely linked.

Q **How did you relate to the customer base and how did that work in practice?**

A I've not found another role where I had the ability to speak directly to people who were at the 'coal face' and then have the opportunity to influence how we should work to meet their challenges and satisfy their expectations. For instance, at peak times such as Christmas we were given the chance to work in-store when it was extremely busy and this gave me insights into how critical the IT service was and how it impacted customers when things went wrong. It was an eye-opener to be at a large store experiencing a major outage and seeing staff fetching prices to till points and using calculators to add up peoples' shopping. Some customers just left their baskets and walked out which meant bad business for us.

Whilst I always supported and defended my teams, it had to be in the context of the customers' viewpoint and experiences.

Q **What do you see as the role of processes and tools in terms of helping – or hindering – how you did your job?**

A The first thing I learned was that if the tools don't support your processes then you will always have an uphill battle. People, often acting as heroes, will sometimes get you out of a tight spot but this will, over time, wear them down. The core processes of Incident and Change Management were fairly mature but we struggled with Problem Management as it wasn't being given the right degree of steer and there were several hundreds of problems with a small focus rather than a few problems with a dedicated focus. This meant we spent a lot of time fixing the same incidents at the service desk rather than someone working hard to address the root causes. Putting more emphasis on Problem Management following completion of an ITSM review saw a new style of working that targeted key areas to be tackled by quickly identifying the root cause and thus reducing the volume of incidents. I cannot emphasise strongly enough how positive an impact the sudden removal of incidents that the team knew would occur over and over again had on my service desk analysts.

Q **What problems and issues got in the way of being able to do the job to its full potential?**

A Poorly planned projects and first-line staff turnover always created difficulties, especially when the desk was not seen as being fundamental to IT success – which it now is. It was important that leadership and direction came from the top and was filtered down to everyone as if this wasn't done effectively then 'saying and doing' were not aligned and caused issues.

Skill levels on the desk were initially a challenge until I introduced a skills matrix where people were formally recognised in appraisals for increasing their skills in one area or learning new skills as part of a career plan.

Q **How has the experience of doing that job helped you with your IT career and to get other jobs?**

A Having the insight from an operational level has been invaluable to me, firstly as a project manager and then as an ITSM consultant. This is because I knew how low-quality or poorly planned projects affected the business and the people trying to support them and so I could avoid making those mistakes. Being able to refer to real-life situations with customers is something they really value as it isn't just theoretical knowledge but something borne out of having the scars of experience.

THE WORK OF THE SERVICE DESK MANAGER OF A HIGH-STREET BANK

Q **What was your job title?**

A Service Desk Manager – Group IT.

Q **You were responsible for creating a single service desk where there were previously nine separate ones. How did the new service desk come about?**

A A series of mergers had caused us to launch a major service transformation programme in which a single, consolidated help desk was a key part of the brief.

Consolidating so many help desks into one was a new experience for us all and it was teamwork that really drove it forwards. This involved setting up a first- and second-line support team of around 36 people covering everything including the desktop estate and ATMs. The scope of the ITSM project saw the introduction of a new toolset and associated processes for Incident, Change, Problem, Release and Service Request Management.

Q **What background did you have before running the service desk?**

A I was a Regional Support Manager (PCs and servers), managing a small team of infrastructure support personnel and also getting my hands dirty at a technical level. This was a big leap into a people-management role in a customer service team.

Q **What previously acquired knowledge, skills and experience were of most value and how did you go about setting up a team?**

A A sense of humour definitely helped – working in a target-driven environment can be stressful. It was a team effort based on a formally defined project to establish the operation, build the telephony solution and IVR, build the operator toolset, recruit and train the team and I had done some of those things before. The next thing was to concentrate on meeting the targets we had designed. Had we sized the team right? Had we got the working patterns right? Both things that would wake you up in the morning. Poring over statistics to spot how things might be improved is one thing, speaking to the team members AND the internal customers being supported is another. It was that which proved so important, and ultimately rewarding – communication was the key.

Though the manager has individual responsibility and accountability, it is vital to have a great team around you. Selection of the right immediate reports (team supervisors) was essential. Over time this morphed from being the 'absorbed' helpdesk leads to newly recruited experts; selection of the right people with the right experience, open-mindedness and desire to build something new and successful in this field was vital. The recruits had not all previously worked on a service desk either – some came from the high-street branches – but a combination of technical knowledge, enthusiasm and great interpersonal skills was vital. Getting the right people (ultimately) made the manager's role enjoyable, to the point where it became a pleasure to come to work to take on the challenges and seek to achieve (that wonderful management phrase) 'continuous service improvement'.

Q **What was your workload like?**
A We supported every user in the bank, over 9,600 workstations and 655 servers running 230 different applications. There were nine different types of server platform in two big data centres and we handled around 15,000 customer calls a month.

Q **Was this just a Monday to Friday operation for the new team?**
A We initially set up 8am to 8pm working from Monday to Saturday with additional skeleton support for other services, such as ATMs, which needed to be operational around the clock. However, we found that call volumes on Saturday afternoons didn't justify fully manning the desk every weekend, so we were constantly tuning the rota to make sure our coverage matched the expected service need. The operations bridge was manned 24/7 and could take calls on our behalf and refer them to an on-call duty if the need arose. Of course, we had challenging KPIs to meet regardless of the time of day and the call priority.

Q **How did you relate to other managers in IT and what type of meetings did you attend?**
A The relationship with other managers in the IT department was an important one to build for an 'insourced' operation like ours as it was often their teams involved in restoring service in case of an outage. It was vital to have a great working relationship, and from top-down. I would say that

a degree of technical knowledge is helpful to an aspiring service desk manager, but their interpersonal skills are very probably more important. Being able to stay calm under pressure is also vitally important.

Initially, within our service management operation we had a separate problem management function; the team looking to drive root-cause fixes and identify problem trends. The team's leader had to be a very close ally – someone to trust and work closely with. Next up was the service introduction team manager, as new services coming on stream had an immediate impact on the desk and could have been significant. Were our agents equipped with the right knowledge to handle incidents related to the new services? Was the training right? Was the 'expert toolset' set up to assist them? Had we got the right route into 'third tier' support? What was the expected level of incident calls going to be? Would it have expected 'spikes' of impact? Would that necessitate additional staffing or changes to working rotas? All these questions needed examining with the other managers in our IT peer group.

Q **How did you relate to the customer base and how did that work in practice?**

A Showing good dashboard service metrics are fine, but building true customer satisfaction was critical. From incident management surveys we began to identify areas for improvement – getting the customer on-side. Doing that was down to making sure they had real understanding of what we were trying to do for them with the resources we had. From speaking to team managers in areas who had previously complained about service, we built a network of local incident co-ordinators in larger departments. For example in contact centres, instead of people experiencing a service outage and 30 calls being raised by its agents (yes, that used to happen), we would get a nominated individual to raise one incident ticket, and then ensure the correct priority was assigned to the 'ticket', right from the off. By explaining the concept to the business area first hand, getting them to see the desk in operation and showing them how explaining their issue clearly would speed up the overall fix, real strides were made in the desk's service proposition.

Q **What do you see as the role of processes and tools in terms of helping – or hindering – how you did your job?**

A Great processes and tools are incredibly important to a successful service desk. You need a capable and reliable telephony system to handle volumes; a clear IVR to direct calls to the right teams correctly (without a myriad of options!); a reliable and configurable incident recording toolset with workflow for resolving areas (seeing those systems develop in the last 15 years has been fascinating, many now work very well almost out of the box – it was not always so!), great reporting from that system was important too in order to readily generate metrics such as call 'bounces' between resolver groups and ticket 'wait' times – all important feeds to OLAs. The facility to record calls is genuinely valuable too, to aid training of agents and to assist with dispute resolution. (I've learned that latterly; when this particular desk operation started we didn't have that luxury. Of course, screen recording is readily available now too.)

Regarding processes – the areas involved in incident resolution have to understand them. They must be clear and unambiguous, but not necessarily set in stone. On occasions they may need a bit of bending – we initiated something called a 'broken process' review which looked at whether what we did matched the customer experience or not.

Q **What problems and issues got in the way of being able to do the job to its full potential?**

A There will always be problems and issues with a new operation. When launching, you must promote it and that in itself builds an expectation. Mouse mats, flyers, emails, printed guides, posters for the user community can set you up for a fall, especially with many new recruits managing the incidents. We staggered the call take-on by technical discipline (PC desktop, branches, ATMs, call centres) which helped, but when the user community is used to calling their old specific, dedicated service but then gets someone clearly brand new to it, the experience has the immediate potential to be worse. To lessen this, we ensured that some experts were readily on hand to be called upon; AND worked hard on incident classification and integration with an expert system (a knowledge base) to suggest 'first-time' resolutions. But there's still no real replacement for experience.

My service desk was also the front line for a new total fix service, requiring the 'expert resolver groups' to be familiar with processes and the new incident recording tool. Some of those areas took time to understand their responsibilities, possibly keener to deliver their new system, for example, than provide support on an old one. How did we fix that? We got the worst offenders to see the desk first hand, spending time in the shoes of the tier 1 guys to appreciate the challenges they faced. It was a real eye-opener for many people to 'get' service.

Another challenge was sizing the team. Various metrics were used to help with the calculations, but justifying additional members to support new systems or even to replace leavers was often a real challenge which needed support. Motivating the team to achieve targets was 'entertaining', and there was a balance to be struck between hitting call answer times and staffing levels, and then achieving a low call-handling time versus a high first-time fix rate. Many service desks achieve this by taking password and account-lock-out calls, but when those reduce, say by introduction of 'single sign-on' systems and self-service password resets, it can have a big impact on required staffing. Maintaining the required senior management focus on the importance of the service desk when it was trying to trim budgets was also a challenge.

Q **How has the experience of doing that job helped you with your IT career and to get other jobs?**

A There is no doubt that spending four years in a service desk manager role equipped me for career progression. Skills in people management, supplier relationship management and customer management, plus diplomacy, objectivity, communication, training, time management, assertiveness, even crisis management – well, many skills had to be developed and refined. And being involved in technical issue resolution (problem management reviews, etc.) also increased my technical knowledge and understanding.

I am still immensely proud to have been involved in setting up a service desk – applying a design I had input to, tuning it and then ultimately hitting what seemed incredibly aggressive targets was superb. One of the best bits, though, was recruiting relative youngsters who clearly had a talent into their first IT role on 'Tier 1' with the promise of it being THEIR career springboard, and then after three or four years actually seeing it happen. Several rapidly progressed to quite senior technician roles, and still even remain friends today.

Why did I change roles myself? Well, I felt four years was plenty. It's a rewarding job, but a tough one. All the skills and knowledge I learned I have subsequently used – and still use today, though more in a consultative role than as a line manager. The pleasure is that when I advise new companies about service desk design, I am speaking from the position of a lot of real experience, not just from doing an ITIL exam or two. I lose count of how many times I can make a point and back it up with a real example. You don't just learn that, you earn it.

APPENDIX

SERVICE DESK SUPERVISOR INTERVIEWS: SOURCES OF EVIDENCE AGAINST THE ESSENTIAL CRITERIA

Criteria	Source(s) of evidence
Meet the organisation's management competencies	Scenario
Experience of managing an IT Service Desk or Service Support Team in a large complex organisation and across a range of services	Interview
ITILv3 Foundation certificate or the Specialist certificate in Service Desk and Incident Management. Knowledge of ITIL processes and how they impact on the role of the service desk, specifically Incident Management, Problem Management, Service Request Management and Change Management	Interview
Experience of using a Service Desk call logging and tracking system	Interview
Shows an understanding of the purpose and composition of Service Level Agreements and the relationship between an SLA, OLA and a contract for the supply of services	Interview

(Continued)

Criteria	Source(s) of evidence
Can acquire information and identify gaps in the available information required to understand a problem or situation and devise means of remedying such gaps	Scenario and/or occupational test
Has a detailed knowledge of the types of services provided by the IT department and the landscape of the underpinning processes and IT infrastructure (hardware, applications, databases, operating systems, local area networks, etc.)	Interview
Has excellent oral and written communication skills and is able to work at all levels of the organisation	Interview Letter of application and the application form
Is able to influence and persuade across functions where there is no direct line of authority	Interview and presentation
Is familiar with a range of operating system environments, such as Windows, MAC OS, UNIX	Interview
Experience of using remote tools	Interview

INCIDENT MANAGER INTERVIEWS: SOURCES OF EVIDENCE AGAINST THE ESSENTIAL CRITERIA

Criteria	Source(s) of evidence
Experience of providing IT support in a large organisation	Interview
ITILv3 Foundation certificate or equivalent. Knowledge of ITIL processes and how they impact on the role of the service desk specifically Incident Management, Problem Management, Service Request Management and Access Management	Interview
Experience of using a Service Desk call logging and tracking system	Interview
Experience of handling user administration requests (email, identity and access and resource allocation) at a routine level	Interview
Shows an understanding of the purpose and composition of Service Level Agreements and the relationship between an SLA, OLA and a contract for supply of services	Interview
Has good analytical and problem solving skills	Scenario and/ or occupational test
Has a broad knowledge of the types of services provided by the IT department and the landscape of the underpinning processes and IT infrastructure (hardware, applications, databases, operating systems, local area networks, etc.)	Interview

(Continued)

Criteria	Source(s) of evidence
Has excellent oral and written communication skills and is able to work at all levels of the organisation	Interview Letter of application and the application form
Is familiar with a range of operating system environments, such as Windows, MAC OS, UNIX	Interview

BCS
The
Chartered
Institute
for IT

Where is your career going?

Map it out with our free personal development plan

pdp.bcs.org

BCS, The Chartered Institute for IT, First Floor Block D North Star House North Star Avenue Swindon SN2 1F
T +44 (0) 1793 417 424 Online enquiries www.bcs.org/contact **www.bcs.o**
© The British Computer Society (Registered charity no. 292786) 20

If you require this document in accessible format please call +44 (0) 1793 417 (

INDEX